CULTURE SMART!

CZECH REPUBLIC

THE ESSENTIAL GUIDE TO CUSTOMS & CULTURE

KEVAN VOGLER

KUPERARD

"The real voyage of discovery consists not in
seeking new landscapes, but in having new eyes."

Adapted from Marcel Proust, *Remembrance of Things Past*.

ISBN 978 1 78702 292 8

British Library Cataloguing in Publication Data
A CIP catalogue entry for this book is available
from the British Library

First published in Great Britain
by Kuperard, an imprint of Bravo Ltd
59 Hutton Grove, London N12 8DS
Tel: +44 (0) 20 8446 2440
www.culturesmart.co.uk
Inquiries: publicity@kuperard.co.uk

Design Bobby Birchall
Printed in Turkey

The Culture Smart! series is continuing to expand.
All Culture Smart! guides are available as e-books, and many
as audio books. For further information and latest titles visit
www.culturesmart.co.uk

ABOUT THE AUTHOR

KEVAN VOGLER is a Canadian teacher, consultant, and graphic designer who has been living in his adopted homeland of the Czech Republic for more than fifteen years. After graduating in graphic design and illustration and visual communications at Grant MacEwan University in Edmonton, Alberta, Kevan moved to the Czech Republic in 2004. He lives in the country's second-largest city, Brno, home of his Czech partner, where he worked as an English-language teacher and communications consultant to many Czech organizations and private clients, providing English courses and editorial services. He now works in social media and communication and in his free time hosts "Beyond Prague," an online Web site dedicated to the discovery and appreciation of all things Czech.

CONTENTS

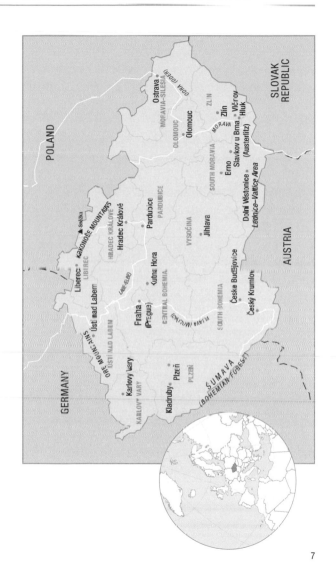

This Culture Smart! guide to the Czech Republic
is designed to give you some insight into the spirit
and worldview of the Czech people. By the time the
thirtieth anniversary of the fall of Communism took
place in late 2019, a seemingly endless stream of
tourists had found their way to Prague and some of
the county's better known tourist attractions. How
many left with a deeper understanding of the culture
is impossible to say.

Lamentably, even this long after the fall of the old
regime, a number of preconceptions about the Czechs
and their culture persist, and many arrive knowing
little more than the old stereotypes about Czech beer
being cheap and the women beautiful. That lack of
knowledge has led to frustration among Czechs, most
of whom are well educated and well informed about
the world around them, and who in turn sometimes
view all tourists as being cut from the same cloth.

Czechs of all classes value education and culture,
and it is never safe to assume that you can tell
someone's status from their appearance. The Czechs
typically come across as rather reserved at first.
However, beneath the layers of social reserve they
are a deeply sincere and caring people. It's a side
most visitors never get to see unless they are alert to
it, but it is visible every time an indifferent-seeming
teenager gets up to give their streetcar seat to an
elderly person, or a senior citizen stops to coo at a

baby in a carriage. Those fortunate enough to make friends with Czechs see it in the fierce loyalty they have for their friends and intimate family. Once a Czech calls someone a friend—and it won't happen overnight—that friendship can last forever.

The Czechs are also deeply, darkly funny, with a distinctive, many-layered sense of humor. They are a people who have made laughing through tears a national survival strategy.

This book introduces you to the customs, values, and attitudes of a remarkable people, and the role of historical and current events in shaping these. It describes Czech life at home and in the workplace and offers practical advice on what to expect and how to behave in unfamiliar social situations. A generation of young Czechs has been born and raised completely free of the old regime, and the number of expatriates putting down roots here has grown significantly. These two factors alone have driven significant change in Czech culture, which this guide explores.

Visiting the Czech Republic will always be worthwhile—its natural bounty and incredible sights are enough to satisfy any aesthete's need for beauty. But the real rewards will come for the visitor who cares enough to try to get inside the culture, beyond the reserve, to the complex corners of the Czech soul.

Official Name	Czech Republic (Česká republika)	Founded on January 1, 1993, when Czechoslovakia split into the Czech Republic and Slovakia.
Capital City	Prague (Praha)	Population: 1.3 million (capital city), 2.7 million (metropolitan area)
Other Major Cities	Brno (capital of Moravia). Population: c. 400,000	Ostrava, Plzeň, Olomouc
Area	30,450 sq. miles (78,866 sq. km)	
Borders	Austria, Germany, Poland, Slovakia	Longest border is with Germany: 503 miles (810 km)
Climate	Continental/temperate with four distinct seasons	Summer temperatures can reach the 95°F–104°F (35°C–40°C) range. Fall and spring are typically mild. Winters can be very cold depending on the region.
Currency	Czech crown (koruna)	The smallest currency unit in circulation is the one crown coin.
Population	10.7 million	One of the lowest birthrates in the world
Ethnic Makeup	63.7% Czech, 4.9% Moravian, 0.1% Silesian, with remainder made up of other or undeclared ethnicity	Significant minorities include Ukrainians, Slovaks, Vietnamese, Russians, Poles, Germans, Bulgarians, Romanians, and Roma (Gypsies).
Language	Czech	West Slavic language

Religion	72% no religious affiliation, 21% Christian (primarily Catholic), 7% non-Christan minorities	Considered to be one of the least religious nations in the world.
Government	Parliamentary democracy	President elected by public vote. Prime minister appointed by president.
Media	Main national newspapers: *Mladá fronta Dnes, Lidové noviny, Hospodářské noviny, Právo*	The Czech Republic ranked 40th on the World Press Freedom Index in 2021.
Media: English Language	Radio Prague. *The Prague Post, Prague Daily Monitor, Brno Daily*	Foreign-language print media available in most large centers. Most hotels have BBC or CNN for televised English-language news. Many also have Wi-Fi.
Electricity	230 volts, 50 Hz	US appliances require adapters/converters.
DVD/Video/ Television	Television is fully digital.	Video is largely gone and DVDs are getting rarer. Streaming services have become the norm.
Internet Domain	.cz	
Telephone	Country code: 420 There are no regional or area codes.	To call the US or Canada, dial 001 + the area code and the phone number.
Time Zones	Central European Time (CET). End Mar. to end Oct., Central European Summer Time (CEST).	One hour ahead of UTC (GMT) and six hours ahead of EST. CEST is GMT + 2.

CHAPTER ONE

LAND & PEOPLE

Occupying a geographical footprint of 30,451 square miles (78,867 sq. km) in the heart of Central Europe, and with a population of more than 10,700,000 people, the Czech Republic is a developed country with high standards of education and healthcare. It also ranks among the top ten safest places in the world to live in. The modern state came into being in 1993 with the peaceful split of Czechoslovakia into separate Czech and Slovak republics.

This landlocked country has a long history of human habitation reaching back to the Paleolithic era, a remarkable diversity of geographical landscapes for its size, and sixteen UNESCO World Heritage Sites within its borders.

The usual point of entry for visitors is the capital, Prague. In 2020, the city's metropolitan area was home to around 2.7 million people. Other major cities with populations of 100,000 or more include Brno, Olomouc, Ostrava, and Plzeň.

The Czech Republic's architectural heritage is rich and varied, representing the different styles and artistic movements through the ages and the skills of generations of architects and artists. In many places around the country you can find Baroque, Gothic, and Renaissance structures happily juxtaposed with Classicist, Secessionist, and Modernist buildings to create some unforgettable urban vistas. Within the mix, you'll also find remnants of Socialist Realism and modern Brutalist styles, among others. You could be taking in the lofty medieval spires of Prague's historic center one day, enjoying one of the many fairs at Brno's Modernist exhibition center the next, and then moving on to the stark, epic expanse of the old Vítkovice steel mill in Ostrava, which stands as a testament to that city's industrial past.

The official language, Czech, belongs to the Czech–Slovak subgroup of the West Slavic language group. It encompasses the Czech and Slovak languages as well as the Moravian dialects of Czech. These are grouped together due to their high degree of mutual intelligibility.

In the broadest sense, the Czech Republic can be divided into three geographical regions, the largest of which is Bohemia (Čechy) in the west. The greater part of the east of the country consists of Moravia (Morava), while a small section of the northeast is Moravian Silesia (Moravské Slezsko). While these are historical divisions, many contemporary Czechs still use them as a way to define their own ancestry and origins among their compatriots.

Dramatic sandstone formations in the Bohemian Paradise (Český ráj), a protected landscape area.

GEOGRAPHY AND CLIMATE

There is a variety of landscapes to explore within the
Czech Republic. The low mountains and rolling hills in
the Polish and Slovak border regions and the Vysočina
highlands region in the south-central part of the country
contrast with the well-cultivated agricultural areas of
South Bohemia and the wine country of South Moravia.
Important rivers include the Labe (Elbe), Vltava
(Moldau), Morava, and Odra (Oder). Slovakia ended up
with most of the mountains when Czechoslovakia split,
but the Czech Republic still boasts several high peaks
in the Krkonoše (Giant) mountain range, including
Sněžka at 5,200 feet (1,600 m) above sea level. There

are floodplains, grassland, karst, steppe, wetland, and woodland environments. As many of these areas are protected, they are usually in good condition.

The Czech climate is temperate, with four distinct seasons. Spring, though March and April, is fairly mild, and temperatures can still be a bit unpredictable. While daytime highs of 46–57°F (8–14°C) are not unusual, it still is possible for the temperature to drop into the freezing range. May is distinctly warmer, with many flowers and trees in bloom and daytime highs of 60–77°F (15–25°C) being the norm.

Summer temperatures average around 70–80°F (20–27°C), though heatwaves in July and August reaching 95–104°F (35–40°C) are not uncommon.

The weather in fall can be quite variable, from warm and pleasant to chilly and wet. From mid-September to early October, the phenomenon of "*babí léto*" (Grandma Summer) can take place; this is generally equivalent to an "Indian Summer" in North America, with uncharacteristically mild temperatures and sunny days for the time of year.

The temperature tends to drop noticeably through October to an average of around 48–57°F (10–14°C) with an unpredictable mix of sunny and rainy weather.

Winter is generally gray and wet in most urban areas, with the first snows falling in some areas by mid-November. Temperatures through November, January, and February tend to be chilly and average around the freezing mark or a bit below.

There are few extremes in Czech weather, although the precipitation levels combined with the low-lying

Day breaks over the meandering Labe River.

terrain can lead to widespread and extremely damaging floods, the worst of which took place in 2002.

Since approximately 2015, the Czech Republic has been experiencing significantly drier conditions than usual. This trend has also been seen in Poland and Slovakia and is a situation that weighs on the minds of people in all three nations for the threat it poses to agriculture, water supplies, and entire communities.

ETHNIC GROUPS

The Czech Republic is ethnically rather homogeneous. This is particularly evident when compared to its traditionally "Western" neighbors, Austria and Germany, which have taken in immigrants and refugees from many countries for some time and have well-instituted programs for their integration.

The country's current ethnic face is definitively European, with native Slavic groups making up the majority. In the most recent census the top three ethnicities by a large margin were Czech, Moravian, and Slovak. Slovaks are generally seen very favorably by Czechs and there is a sibling-like closeness between them. Both are Western Slavs and their languages are, as we've seen, to a large degree mutually intelligible. If there is a difference historically between the two, it's that while both peoples were subjects of the Austro-Hungarian Empire, the Slovaks were more influenced by Hungarian and the Czechs by Germanic culture. This has led to the stereotypes of the Czechs being more emotionally restrained and orderly in their affairs while the Slovaks are supposed to be more relaxed and free in showing their emotions. While the Czechs have the reputation of being a bit reserved at first toward outsiders, the Slovaks are said to be much quicker to welcome newcomers into their midst. Religion, primarily Catholicism, is much more widespread among Slovaks than among Czechs.

Other ethnicities listed in the 2011 Census include Ukrainian, Polish, Vietnamese, German, Russian, Silesian, and Roma (Gypsies). Outside the official census results, the population is known also to contain Belarusian, Bulgarian, Croatian, Hungarian, Ruthenian, Greek, and Serbian minorities.

The Czech government has formally recognized and extended privileges to certain minority groups through the Government Council for National Minorities. As of 2020, it had recognized fourteen such groups: Belarusian, Bulgarian, Croatian, Hungarian, German, Polish, Roma, Ruthenian, Russian, Greek, Slovak, Serbian, Ukrainian, and Vietnamese. Each group can nominate one or two representatives to sit on the council and advise the government on setting policy toward national minorities in the country.

A BRIEF HISTORY

There has been continuous human activity and settlement in the region since the Stone Age, and there are significant archaeological sites near the village of Dolní Věstonice in the southeast. Study of the Paleolithic settlement there has yielded important insights into life on the Continent in that period.

Excavations have produced the oldest evidence of ceramic and textile technologies. A kiln and a number of fired ceramic animal figurines, as well as the famed Venus of Dolní Věstonice, were found in 1925, which radio-carbon dating shows to have been made between roughly 27,000 and 20,000 BCE, making them the oldest known ceramic artefacts in the world.

Imprints of textiles on ceramic tiles at the site show that not only had the weavers of the time experimented with and developed a number of different weaving techniques, but that hunters

The Venus of Dolní Věstonice.

sometimes used nets for hunting as well as spears.

A grave at the site containing three youths sheds light on burial practices that existed at the time.

Also among the artefacts at Dolní Věstonice were seashells from the Mediterranean— indicators of whom the people of the settlement traded with.

As well as Stone Age sites, there are also numerous sites from the following Bronze and Iron Ages.

Early Tribes and Romans

The oldest recorded settlers in the present-day Czech Republic were a Celtic tribe called the Boii, from which the name Bohemia stems (Latin *Boiohaemum*). The Boii lived in the region from the fourth century BCE and were eventually joined by Germanic tribes who established the Marcomanni kingdom north of the Danube River.

Confronted by these powerful barbarians, the Romans built forts and military settlements in what is today South Moravia to support their offensives during the Marcomannic Wars (166–180 CE). Ultimately the wars ended in victory for Rome, but it was a limited one that saw the Danube retained as the northern frontier of Roman territory, and the Romans never formally expanded their empire into what would become the Czech Republic.

Rome's influence in the region is thought to cover the period c. 50–30 BCE to 375 CE. As it didn't establish permanent settlements, many considered that it had had little cultural impact. However, had it not been for the Romans, the long and proud tradition of Czech winemaking might never have come about. Evidence of this came to light during study of a Roman fort near the village of Pasohlávky in 1926, when a vine pruning knife was unearthed.

Great Moravia

Slavic peoples penetrated the territories of present-day Moravia and Slovakia in the sixth century CE. In the ninth century the kingdom of Great Moravia was founded in the eastern part of the region, with Christianity finding its way into the mix of religions practiced at the time and eventually becoming dominant. The Moravian state is first mentioned in historical documents in 811. Its first known ruler was Mojmír I, who ruled from c. 820/830 to 846. Through the interference of Louis the German, king of East Francia (and grandson of Charlemagne), Mojmír was deposed and replaced by Rastislav.

The period under Rastislav I was important culturally. The first alphabet of the Slavic language, known as Old Church Slavonic, was created by the Byzantine missionaries Cyril and Methodius, and the Bible and much ecclesiastical literature was translated into that language. Rastislav sought to minimize the influence of

Frankish missionaries by increasing the number of Moravian priests trained to minister in Old Slavonic. Cyril and Methodius arrived in Moravia in 863 and had completed their work by late 866.

Saints Cyril and Methodius. Modern tapestry in St. Martin's Cathedral, Bratislava, Slovakia.

Rastislav reigned from 846 to 870. Initially a vassal of East Francia, he turned against his Frankish overlords in the early 850s. Aided by Bulgarian forces, the Moravians were able to defend their territory against a number of Frankish sieges.

Another key player during this period was Louis' eldest son, Carloman, whom he put in charge of bringing the Moravians to heel. After a failed invasion of Moravia in 856, Carloman struck an alliance with Rastislav and turned on Louis. It was an alliance that saw Carloman take much of his father's territory for himself.

Rastislav's reign ended abruptly when he was betrayed by his nephew, Svatopluk, and handed over to the Franks. This was the result of a deal Svatopluk had made with Carloman behind Rastislav's back, and it put Moravia firmly back in Frankish hands.

In the early 870s relations between Svatopluk I and East Francia soured and fighting for control over Moravia resumed. The conflict ended with the departure of the Franks and the signing of a peace treaty in 874.

During Svatopluk's reign, from 870 to 894, Great Moravia reached its maximum size and political influence, and included areas that today are parts of the Czech Republic, Hungary, Poland, and Slovakia. Svatopluk cultivated good relations with the Holy See in Rome and in 880 Moravia and its people were granted papal protection. After Pope Stephen V prohibited the use of Old Church Slavonic in Moravia in favor of Latin, Svatopluk expelled the Byzantine missionaries in 886.

The last king of Great Moravia was Mojmír II, the son of Svatopluk I. Mojmír ruled from 894 to c. 906/907. Moravia was being pulled apart by internal friction, with many areas that had been acquired by Svatopluk seeking to leave. These included Bohemia, a duchy of Moravia under Svatopluk, which successfully broke away in 895.

Moravia fell to Magyar invaders in the early tenth century, and its lands were divided between Bohemia and Hungary.

The Kingdom of Bohemia

Having broken away from Moravia in 895 and inherited a portion of the fallen kingdom's territory, Bohemia was set to write the next chapter in Czech history.

Early on, Bohemia was ruled by the homegrown Přemyslid dynasty. This dynasty, which ruled the Czech lands until 1306, was founded by the semilegendary Princess Libuše, sometimes called the Mother of the

Czech Nation. According to the most famous retelling of the legend, written at the height of the nineteenth-century Czech national revival by Alois Jirásek, Libuše foretold the founding of Prague standing on the hill at Vyšehrad and saying, "Behold, I see a great city, whose fame will touch the stars."

Princess Libuše ruled the Czech lands wisely and her people were happy, as Jirásek tells it, until two quarreling clansmen questioned her judgment because she was a woman. Incensed, she chastised them for not appreciating her sensitive style of ruling and told them to find her a husband who would rule in her place. She even told them where to find him and what he would be—a simple plowman (*Přemysl*). When they returned with Přemysl, the two were wed, thus founding the Přemyslid dynasty.

The first Přemyslid prince, Bořivoj, is said to have built Prague Castle high above the Vltava River in around 880, transferring power there from the fortress of Vyšehrad. However, historical documentation shows that the castle was in existence several decades before Bořivoj's time. During the Přemyslid reign, the Czech state managed to maintain titular sovereignty, despite its incorporation into the Holy Roman Empire in 950. The savage murder of the pious Prince Wenceslas (Václav) by his pagan brother Boleslav in 935 created a Christian martyr and a symbol of Czech nationalism, and Wenceslas became the patron saint of Bohemia.

Bořivoj's sons, particularly Spytihněv I, continued their father's work. Spytihněv oversaw the completion of the heart of the Czech state, a circle of land radiating 18 miles (30 km) in all directions from Prague.

Spytihněv's reign was a critical time in the development of Prague. By the end of the ninth century, it had become the seat of political power and culture. It then became the center of religious authority when a bishopric was established there in 973. As the Czech state has grown and developed, Prague has always retained its place as the heart of cultural, political, and religious power. No other European capital can rival that level of continuity.

In 1029 Moravia became a fiefdom of Bohemia, and in the twelfth century Bohemia became a kingdom.

By the turn of the thirteenth century, Bohemia was in a rapid growth cycle, with numerous towns being established as centers for crafts and trades. It also acquired a level of prestige due to the wealth it derived from a rich deposit of silver lying between the cities of Jihlava and Kutná Hora. The latter city was, at its height, the second-most important city in Bohemia after Prague itself. It was given the title of a royal city and the state mint was established there. For its place in Czech history, Kutná Hora is listed as a UNESCO World Heritage Site and is a very popular tourist destination. Under Otakar II, who reigned from 1253 to 1278, the Czech kingdom expanded to include territory in modern-day Austria and Slovenia.

Kneeling on the left, Charles IV, King of Bohemia and Holy Roman Emperor. Detail on votive panel, c. 1370.

The Přemyslid dynasty died out after the murder of Wenceslas III, but the Czech lands reached a high point in power and prestige under Charles IV of the House of Luxembourg, which had married into the Přesmyslids in the early fourteenth century, who reigned from 1346 to 1378. Charles was elected Holy Roman Emperor in 1355 and chose Prague as the Imperial residence. He rebuilt and beautified the city and founded a number of notable institutions, including Charles University, the oldest university in central Europe.

Charles was succeeded on the Bohemian throne by his son, Wenceslas IV, who ruled from 1378 to 1419. The reign of Wenceslas took place at the same time as the great Papal Schism of 1378–1417. This event saw two papal claimants, based in Rome and Avignon respectively, vying for legitimacy as head of the Church. European rulers, nobility, and clergy were forced to back one or the other party.

Church and State

Wenceslas backed the Avignon papacy, and this put him at odds with the Prague archdiocese, which backed the Rome papacy. Further friction between the king and the archdiocese came from the king's desire to acquire the holdings of the wealthy and influential Benedictine abbey at Kladruby, near Plzeň. The king decreed that no new abbot was to be elected when the incumbent died.

Matters came to a head in 1393 when the Vicar General of the Prague archidocese, John of Nepomuk, in defiance of the king's order, not only encouraged the election of an abbot but also confirmed the new abbot personally. This act enraged Wenceslas and he had the Vicar General imprisoned, tortured, and drowned in the Vltava River. The king faced a serious backlash from the Czech nobility for this deed. John of

St. John of Nepomuk. Statue on Charles Bridge, Prague.

Nepomuk was seen as a martyr and was eventually made a saint in 1729. Statues of him are very common around the Czech Republic today.

The king's poor relationship with the Church extended to his willingness to support the calls for Church reform of the Czech theologian and philosopher Jan Hus, and he refused to comply with demands from Rome to denounce Hus and his followers as heretics.

In May, 1415, Hus was brought before the ecumenical Council of Constance—convened mainly to end the Papal Schism—and charged with heresy. After refusing to recant, he was condemned to death and burned at the stake in Constance on July 6, 1415. The remainder of Wenceslas IV's reign was overshadowed by events leading up to the Hussite Wars that broke out in 1419, shortly before his death.

The Hussite Wars (1419–36)

Jan Hus is regarded as one of the earliest religious reformers, second only to the English theologian John Wycliffe. In fact, he was greatly influenced by the writings of Wycliffe and called for many of the same reforms, such as a reduction in the hierarchy and opulence that had grown in the Church's upper ranks. Hus and his words resonated deeply with Bohemians and he became very popular with the people. In the wake of his death, his followers organized themselves into what would become known as the Hussite movement—a forerunner of Protestantism.

Things did not go well for the Hussites immediately after the death of Hus. This was largely because

Jan Hus preaching (left). Battle between Hussites and crusaders (right). Jenský Codex, fifteenth century.

Wenceslas, who had ambitions to be elected Holy Roman Emperor, changed his views on Hus and his ideas on reform and ceased to support them. Where once the followers of Hus had held many high positions in government, the king did everything he could to remove them from their positions after Hus' execution.

In June 1419, a group of Hussites led by the priest Jan Želivský stormed the New Town Hall in Prague and threw several town councilors and the king's representatives out of the windows onto the street below, killing them in the process. This act became known as the first "Defenestration of Prague" and it was the event that touched off the Hussite Wars, which raged from 1419 to 1436.

In a nutshell, the Hussite Wars were a series of five crusades against Hussite Bohemia in which the reformist armies led by Jan Žižka held the Catholic Emperor's superior forces at bay. By the mid-fifteenth century, the Catholic Church and the Hussites had reached an uneasy truce, but in 1526 the Austrian-Catholic Habsburgs reconquered Bohemia. When Lutheranism began to penetrate the country the largely Protestant Czech nobility gained in strength.

Habsburg Rule

Relations between the Bohemian nobility and the Habsburgs were tense, to say the least. The second "Defenestration of Prague"—which took place in 1618 and aggravated those already poor relations further—saw three royal Catholic officials tossed from the windows of the Old Royal Palace of Prague Castle. Of the two Prague defenestrations this is the more famous, as it was a prime catalyst for starting the Thirty Years' War that raged in Europe from 1618 to 1648.

Habsburg control in the region was cemented in 1620 with the defeat of the Bohemian nobility at the Battle of White Mountain. Following their defeat—commemorated by a monument on Prague's Old Town Square—the Czechs were forced to convert to Catholicism or leave, a policy that has perhaps led to their being less religious than their neighbors even today. Leading the fight against Protestantism were the Jesuits, who built many new churches in the Baroque style.

The Czech lands remained part of the Habsburg Empire—and were subject to its attendant assimilationist and Germanization policies—until 1918. By the nineteenth century, the Czech language itself was in danger of dying out, with the educated classes speaking and writing German. In 1848, a national revival of language and culture turned political, and the Czechs began demanding greater sovereignty. With the creation of the dual Austro-Hungarian monarchy in 1867, Bohemia was reduced to a province of Austria and nationalist sentiment grew. But the goal of an independent state would not be reached until after the First World War, when the empire dissolved following Austria-Hungary's defeat.

The First Republic

The postwar Treaty of Versailles enshrined the principle of national self-determination, and on October 28, 1918, the sovereign state of Czechoslovakia was founded. Within ten years the so-called First Republic of Czechs and Slovaks, led by President Tomáš Garrigue Masaryk, had become one of the most advanced countries in the world, with one of the most progressive constitutions.

The First Republic is an era for which many Czechs have a deep sense of nostalgia. It was a time when the young nation was swiftly coming into

Tomáš Masaryk in 1925.

its own, and not only was it reaching out to the rest of the world, many other nations were reaching out to it.

The period has been the subject of at least two popular Czech television series in the years since Socialism ended. *Četnické Humoresky* (*Policeman's Humoresques*) followed the adventures of a group of police officers in the city of Brno. The series mixed crime, drama, and comedy, and many of the episodes were based on actual case files from the period. The series premiered in 1997 and ran for three seasons, and is replayed regularly on TV.

První Republika (The First Republic) was a drama series first aired in 2014 and was made for three seasons. It was noted for the authenticity of its costumes and sets and drew many comparisons to the UK's *Downton Abbey* in the historical genre.

Tragically, the First Republic survived little more than twenty years. At the infamous Munich Conference in September 1938, in response to Hitler's territorial demands, Great Britain, France, and Italy agreed to the cession of the northern Czech Sudetenland districts, home to many ethnic Germans, to Nazi Germany. The remainder of Czechoslovakia was invaded and annexed by Germany in March 1939. President Eduard Beneš set up a government-in-exile in London. The Nazi occupation lasted until the end of the Second World War in May 1945.

The Nazi Occupation

After hiving off Slovakia, the Germans turned the rump Czech state into the nominally autonomous Protectorate of Bohemia and Moravia. One of the most notorious events to occur during the occupation followed the assassination of Reinhard Heydrich, Deputy Reich-Protector of Bohemia and Moravia. In 1942, a group of Czech resistance fighters who had been trained in England returned to Prague to carry out the assassination. Although Heydrich was only wounded in the attack, he died a week later of blood poisoning caused by shrapnel lodged in his wounds.

In response, the Gestapo and SS killed as many as 1,000 Czechs suspected of being involved in the assassination and deported 3,000 Jews. But the reprisals did not stop there. In June, just days after Heydrich died, Hitler ordered the liquidation of the small Czech town of Lidice for its alleged role in helping the assassins—a charge that had no basis in fact. Nearly two hundred men and boys over the age of sixteen were shot, while the women were sent to a concentration camp. Young children were sent to another camp. The village was then razed and crops were planted over the area.

The plan to assassinate Heydrich was given the codename Operation Anthropoid. The 2016 film *Anthropoid* was based on the operation and the subsequent destruction of Lidice. The film was shot entirely in Prague, with authentic locations of the historical events often being used as sets.

In addition to dramatic events such as these, ordinary Czechs were deported to work as slave labor in German factories, and Gestapo roundups, arbitrary violence and executions, and near-starvation conditions were everyday occurrences.

Czechoslovakia was liberated by Soviet and American troops in 1945, and a government of national unity was formed under Beneš. The country expelled its two to three million ethnic German citizens, and thousands were killed in the process. The expulsion further worsened relations between Czechoslovakia and Germany and Austria, and groups of expellees and their descendants living outside Czech territory are still lobbying for compensation for lost property. However, most Czechs believe the expulsions were justified because of the suffering experienced under Nazi occupation— suffering that included not only the brutal repression of Czechs but also the deportation and extermination of most of the Roma (Gypsies) and Jews in the country.

Communist Takeover

After the war, by the terms of the deal struck at Yalta in 1945 between Roosevelt, Churchill, and Stalin, Czechoslovakia was placed into the Soviet sphere of influence. Initially working within the postwar democratic political system, the Soviet-backed Communist Party of Czechoslovakia seized complete control in February 1948, forcing the young country behind the Iron Curtain to suffer yet again the indignities of occupation and totalitarianism. Stalinist show trials in the 1950s—conducted to purge the Party of those considered insufficiently supportive of Stalinism— terrorized the populace and led most people to retreat into themselves.

The Suppression of Wartime Heroes

An important chapter of Czechoslovak history was written during the war when a number of men and women escaped their occupied homeland to join the Allied forces in the fight against Hitler. Knowledge of this was suppressed for decades by the Socialist regime that took power in 1948, and many Czechs and Slovaks had no idea of the heroism of their compatriots until the information was made public after the fall of Socialism. The most famous Czech and Slovak fighters in the Allied armies were those who went to Britain to join the Royal Air Force. Czech and Slovak pilots, along with those from Poland, quickly developed a reputation as some of the most determined and fearsome flyers in the RAF.

At first, the Czech and Slovak veterans returned home to a well deserved hero's welcome. However, partly due to the exposure they had had to Western, democratic society during the war, the Socialist regime saw them as a political threat, and systematically suppressed any information about their wartime exploits and marginalized them in Czechoslovak society. Many escaped back to Western countries, while those who remained typically ended up working in the mines or doing other hard, menial labor. The experiences of those pilots, both during the war and at home after the Socialist takeover, were the subject of the 2001 British–Czech film *Tmavomodrý svět* (*Dark Blue World*), directed by the award winning director Jan Svěrák.

The Prague Spring and "Normalization"

In the late 1960s, the Czech Communists led by Alexander Dubček did attempt to lighten the hand of the regime in a reform effort christened the "Prague Spring," but the August 1968 invasion by the armies of

Protesters carry the national flag past a burning tank during the Soviet invasion of Czechoslovakia.

five Warsaw Pact countries ended the experiment of "Socialism With a Human Face." Albania, Romania, and the former Yugoslavia were notable among the Socialist European nations in their support of Czechoslovakia and their refusal to participate in the invasion.

In January 1969, Jan Palach, a student at Charles University, took his own life by self-immolation as a political protest against the Warsaw Pact invasion that had ended the Prague Spring. His death was followed by demonstrations against the Socialist government and the self-immolation of another student, Jan Zajíc, in April of the same year. The acts of protest by Palach and Zajíc still strike a deep chord with Czechs today and tributes are placed at a monument to the men on Prague's Wenceslas Square on the anniversaries of their protests.

Directly on the heels of the Prague Spring came the "Normalization." Broadly speaking, the Normalization covered the period of 1969 to 1987 and started as a move to restore power to the Communist Party and suppress the ideas of reform that Dubček had promoted. However, Normalization grew to affect virtually every aspect of life in Czechoslovakia for nearly two decades.

By early 1969 Dubček had been ousted from the Party and replaced as leader by Gustav Husák. Almost as soon as he was installed, Husák set about purging reformists from all levels of government and consolidating power on himself. He was a more-than-willing puppet for the Communist higher-ups in Moscow and happily toed their line in every regard when it came to running Czechoslovakia.

Husák had planned to win over the populace by increasing the amount and variety of consumer goods available as a way of compensating for the loss of personal freedoms under his government. This worked for a very short time, but by the late 1970s the economy had begun to stagnate and consumer goods were no compensation for a public who couldn't afford them.

In 1977 a human rights group of intellectuals called "Charter 77," which included the playwright Václav Havel, was formed. This led to a harsh crackdown against dissidents.

Economic stagnation and further suppression of personal freedoms continued into the 1980s, breeding cynicism and pessimism, and a poor work ethic—defined by apathy at the workers' level and corruption at the executive level—as well as a black market economy for all the things the regime forbade. It also fostered favoritism and nepotism, which ensured that those with the right connections could get what others could not. In this climate one may find a possible cause for the envy that many Czechs claim is part of their national character.

The light at the end of the tunnel for the Czechs came when Mikhail Gorbachev rose to power in the Soviet Union in 1985. Gorbachev had his own ideas for reform, expressed in the concepts of *perestroika* (restructuring) and *glastnost* (openness). Both principles were at odds with Normalization, which could not survive in the face of them and the hope that they gave to oppressed peoples throughout the Socialist states of Europe. If such changes could be effected at the very heart of Communism, they could certainly be brought about in their own countries.

In 1989, the five Warsaw Pact nations that had participated in the 1968 invasion of Prague formally and publicly extended apologies to Czechoslovakia for having done so.

The Velvet Revolution

Czechoslovakia had continued to languish under Communist rule until 1989, when the decay of the Soviet empire and the decline of the Communist system sparked unrest and demonstrations around Eastern and Central Europe. These culminated in Czechoslovakia in the November '89 demonstrations—under the spiritual guidance of Alexander Dubček and Václav Havel—that led to the fall of the Communist regime. New political parties were formed and legalized, and the Communist Party was stripped of its powers. Havel was appointed president and thousands of prisoners were granted an amnesty. The events were popularly known as the Velvet Revolution.

The Parting of the Ways

Wrangling between politicians in Czechoslovakia's two ethnic constituencies—most notably former Slovak Prime Minister Vladimír Mečiar and former Czech Prime Minister (later president) Václav Klaus—led to a parliamentary decision to divide the country into the Czech Republic and Slovakia (sometimes called the "Velvet Divorce"). A referendum on the issue was never held, but the country was partitioned on January 1, 1993, and Václav Havel was elected president of the Czech Republic. At the time, polls indicated that only 9 percent of the population supported the break. Polls taken two and half decades later showed that more than half of all Czechs and Slovaks felt that the separation had not been beneficial and resented the fact that there had been no referendum on it.

A number of causes have been cited for the breakup. Chief among them were the incompatible visions of Václav Klaus and Vladimír Mečiar about how Czechoslovakia should move forward politically and economically. The Czech part of the country was more developed industrially and financially than the Slovak half, and Klaus wanted rapid privatization of state-held enterprises and economic growth, while Mečiar took a much more cautious approach, fearing that better paid work abroad would attract highly trained professionals away from the Slovak regions.

At the time of the split, both men expressed the view that partition was inevitable. When they were interviewed about this in 2018, on the twenty-fifth anniversary of the event, neither had changed their view.

In spite of the breakup, the people of both nations have maintained their sibling-like closeness.

Since 1993, the Czech Republic has successfully integrated itself into wider multinational structures, including the OECD in 1995, NATO in 1999, the European Union in 2004, and the Schengen Area in 2007.

THE CZECH GOVERNMENT

The Czech Republic is a parliamentary democracy. The head of state is the president and the prime minister is the head of government. The president is elected by direct vote for a five-year term and has limited but very specific powers; the prime minister is appointed by the president. The prime minister appoints and leads a cabinet of seventeen ministers.

View of the Government Office and Prague Castle from the Vltava River.

Parliament consists of two branches, the Chamber of Deputies—the Lower House—and the Senate. Deputies and senators are chosen through public election. For administrative and electoral purposes, the country is divided into fourteen regions, or *kraje*—*kraj* in singular. A *kraj* is equivalent to a state or province.

Václav Havel stepped down as president after ten years in office in the winter of 2003 and was ultimately replaced by former prime minister Václav Klaus, after several contentious rounds of elections.

Václav Klaus held the office of president from 2003 to 2013. His years in office are remembered for a great deal of controversy, particularly over his Euroskeptic views and his denial of global warming and climate change.

Klaus was succeeded by Miloš Zeman, who was the first Czech president to be elected by direct vote. Both Havel and Klaus had been elected by parliament.

Zeman was reelected in 2018 and thus far his presidency has been marked by a tremendous amount of controversy and a general skepticism among many Czechs about his fitness to lead.

Like Klaus before him, Zeman is a Euroskeptic and a climate-change denier. He has drawn much fire from the press and public over his appointment of Slovak-born Andrej Babiš as prime minister in 2017. A number of controversies have surrounded Babiš, both at home and at the EU level, and his legacy as prime minister is certain to be a contentious one among Czechs for years to come.

The unpopularity the Zeman/Babiš government among Czechs was shown in no uncertain terms in June 2019 by public demonstrations against it in Prague and other areas around the country. These were the largest public demonstrations since the Velvet Revolution in 1989.

Following the 2021 parliamentary election, the major political groupings in the country included the center-right ANO Party—led by Andrej Babiš—and Spolu, a center-right leaning coalition of the Civic Democratic Party (ODS), Christian and Democratic Union–Czechoslovak People's Party (KDU-ČSL), and the TOP 09 Party that was formed to give Babiš and his party serious competition in the election.

The remaining parliamentary groups consisted of the centrist Pirates and Mayors—an alliance of the Czech Pirate Party and the Mayors and Independents party (STAN)—and the far-right Freedom and Direct Democracy Party (SPD).

While the Spolu alliance narrowly beat the ANO Party in total votes, ANO still remains the most powerful single party in the Lower House. It could take several months of negotions before a parliament based on the results of the election is formed. How Miloš Zeman choses to influence those negotions will also play a big part in shaping the new Lower House. There is much uncertainty and speculation about how things will pan out at the time of this book going to press.

One of the most significant developments arising from the 2021 election was that, for the first time since the founding of the Czech Republic in 1993, there was no Communist representation in parliament as the far-left Communist Party of Bohemia and Moravia (KSČM) failed to secure enough votes to gain any seats.

THE ECONOMY

Czechoslovakia under Communism had many industrial areas and manufacturing plants, as well as some mining. Much of the heavy industry was located in Slovakia, meaning that after the 1993 split the Czech Republic no longer had a decaying industrial legacy, apart from a few spots in Northern Bohemia and Moravian Silesia. Generally speaking, the Czech Republic has prospered since then.

The Czech economy is strong and highly diversified. The country enjoys solid economic growth along with the lowest unemployment rate in the EU—around 2.0 percent in January 2020—and one of the lowest poverty rates in the OECD. While the COVID-19 pandemic and its associated quarantine measures will leave their mark on the economy and unemployment rate for some time to come, the most immediate threats to continued economic growth are likely to remain workforce shortages and an ageing population.

The largest sector of the economy is services, which make up approximately 60 percent of GDP. Significant among these are ICT, nanotechnology, research and development, software development, and tourism.

Industry accounts for 37 percent of GDP. This sector includes automotive, aerospace, and other transportation equipment manufacture. It also encompasses the production of chemicals, glass, pharmaceuticals, and steel. Some Czech products—such as Škoda cars (owned by Volkswagen since 2000), Pilsner beer, Zetor tractors, and Czech-made streetcars and trolleys (used in cities worldwide)—are internationally famous.

Agriculture still plays a small but important part in the economy, accounting for approximately 2 percent of GDP. Important aspects of Czech agriculture include fruits and vegetables, cereals, hops, oilseeds, viticulture, livestock, and milk.

The country's currency, the Czech crown (koruna) (CZK), has fared well against the dollar and the euro for several years and looks set to continue this trend. While there has been a significant push in recent years by the EU and many in the business community for the country to adopt the euro (many Czech businesses operate in euros) neither the government nor the public seems to be in any hurry to adopt the common currency. On the government side, it's largely been a matter of having euroskeptic presidents like Klaus and Zeman in charge. On the public side, many Czechs are quite attached to the koruna and regard it as one of the last tangible signs of national sovereignty they have left. The European debt crisis in 2009 did much to strengthen public resolve against the euro as Czechs saw their own economy stay strong while many euro-based economies faltered.

In the years since Socialism, the Czech Republic has become a favorite destination for foreign companies. Initially, such companies based themselves in Prague; however, the combination of lower operating costs and well-established talent pools in other urban centers—notably Brno, Ostrava, and Plzeň—resulted in many firms keeping small administrative offices in the capital and moving the larger part of their Czech operations to other cities. In recent years, based on the strength of IT training in Czech post-secondary institutes and the competence of their graduates, many foreign companies have set up their IT support centers in the country.

Testament to Czech IT competence is the Seznam company, which was founded in 1996. Seznam has the distinction of being one of the very few domestically created Internet search engines and portals in the world that can outperform the Web giant Google locally.

CZECHS AROUND THE WORLD

A Czech diaspora can be found in lands around the world, with high concentrations in the midwestern United States and the state of Texas, dating from the nineteenth and early twentieth centuries. The impact of Czech and Slovak immigration on the American Midwest can be seen in the National Czech and Slovak Museum and Library in Cedar Rapids, Iowa. During the Communist era, and especially after 1968, large numbers of dissidents fled the country for points abroad, including the United States, Canada, Australia, and other Western countries. After the fall of Communism many returned to their homeland.

Czechs today continue to emigrate, but not in the numbers once seen. There is, however, a steady stream of human "exports" in the form of top-level athletes, especially hockey and football (soccer) players, with Czechs reaching the apex of global and European competition. Some of the best-known Czech

athletes are tennis star Martina Navratilova (born in
Prague, but who became an American citizen after
defecting in 1975), and National Hockey League
forward Jaromír Jágr, who played for nine NHL teams
as well as the 1998 Olympic gold medal-winning team
and the 2006 Olympic bronze medal-winning team.

The Czech lands throughout history have produced
a very large number of important cultural figures.
Well-known writers of Czech origin include Franz
Kafka (*The Trial, Metamorphosis*), Karel and Josef
Čapek (inventors of the word "robot"), and Milan
Kundera (*The Unbearable Lightness of Being*). Antonín
Dvořák, Bedřich Smetana, Leoš Janáček, and Bohuslav
Martinů represent the most famous Czech composers,
although other classical giants, including Mozart, also
worked and lived in Prague and other cities at various
periods in their lives.

Film is another genre in which Czechs have made
impressive contributions. Two-time Academy Award
winner Miloš Forman (*Amadeus, One Flew Over the
Cuckoo's Nest*), Jiří Menzel (1967 Academy Award
winner, *Closely Watched Trains*), Jan Svěrák (1996
Academy Award winner, *Kolja*), and animator and
short filmmaker Jan Švankmajer are all Czechs who
have achieved the highest levels in their art.

Visual artists include Art Nouveau giant Alfons
Mucha, whose images are immediately recognizable in
posters adorning all manner of Czech establishments.

The Czechs have also produced some of the modern
era's best-known philosophers and statesmen—
by happy coincidence, sometimes in the same

person—including post-Communist Czech president and playwright Václav Havel and philosopher and first president of Czechoslovakia, Tomáš Garrigue Masaryk, who espoused such radical notions as equality for women in the early twentieth century.

Art Nouveau. Allegorical illustration for a Zodiac calendar by Alfons Mucha.

Well before the nineteenth and twentieth centuries, the country was also known for porcelain, ceramics, and especially hand-cut lead crystal. The Czech contribution to architecture is at its best in Prague, where Gothic castle remains mingle with the height of Art Nouveau. Prague is also home to one of the only examples of Cubist architecture, the House of the Black Madonna, now housing the Museum of Czech Cubism.

The Czech contribution to world culture is impossible to measure, but is impressive by any standard, especially given the country's small size and its history of oppression by outside forces. It is a tradition of which the Czechs are justifiably proud and which modern Czechs show every sign of continuing.

CHAPTER TWO

VALUES &
ATTITUDES

It is, of course, difficult to generalize fairly about any group of people, the Czechs being no exception, but it is possible to get a feel for what makes a culture tick by taking a look at what they value in themselves.

In the main, Czech society is very individualistic. While Czech people are perfectly capable of working in teams, they are often just as happy to march to the beat of their own drums. This individualism has the benefit of making them a quite independently minded group, but it also creates a degree of reserve in many, which can make getting to know them at first a bit challenging.

Czech society generally values a high standard of education. There are a number of universities around the country with very good reputations internationally and the country's second-largest city, Brno, is said to be one of the best cities in Europe for student living.

Czech humor tends to be rather dark, with an appreciation of the absurd, reflecting a history spent largely under outside authority. It also plays much on pessimism and envy, two qualities that many Czechs will freely concede exist in abundance in their society.

The Czechs are generally a well-educated, resourceful, and self-sufficient people with a historic knack for coming up with very clever and inventive solutions to problems. There is also a level of humility to them—they aren't given to bragging and don't care for it in others.

As we've seen, Czechs are also typically somewhat reserved and tend not to wear their emotions or beliefs on their sleeves. This can make it a bit difficult to read them at first, but should not be interpreted as unfriendliness. Once you break the ice, there is usually a very easygoing and sincere individual beneath.

EDUCATION

Czech society has placed a high value on education for a very long time. Established in 1348, Prague's Charles University is not only the oldest university in central Europe, it ranks as one of the best in the world.

Historically, this respect for education comes partly from having been under Austro–Hungarian rule for four centuries, with its attendant Germanic regard for academic titles and the status they conferred.

Education continued to be prized among Czechs for many years after the establishment of the First Republic in 1918 and for several years after the end of Socialism in 1989. The reason for this is that until the end of Socialism access to post-secondary education was not open to everyone. Under Socialism your educational options were determined by how well connected you were to the ruling regime. A degree of any sort held much weight in society and was a deciding factor in the quality of work you could expect to secure, as it was a point of pride for many companies to be able to say that all their employees were degree holders.

In the years since the fall of Socialism, the importance of degrees and honorifics has waned in Czech society. This is partly to do with the fact that access to post-secondary education was opened up to the majority of citizens and the number of Czech graduates has rocketed. As university graduates are now quite common, not as much prestige follows them as in previous generations. This fact has not diminished the regard for education in Czech society, but it has led to a trend in which younger degree holders no longer feel the need to display their credentials quite so prominently.

The Baroque Theological Hall of the library of Strahov monastery, Prague.

Many foreign companies based in the country tend to hire Czech staff according to the norms of their own internal corporate cultures rather than those of Czech business culture. Experience and know-how may count for much more than a degree in the globalized Czech business environment of today.

The Czech Republic has enjoyed a stable adult literacy rate of 99 percent for several years, as well as an increasing enrollment of foreign students in its many universities. Since the end of Socialism, the number of Czechs holding post-secondary degrees has risen substantially.

YOUTH RISING

Czech society today is made up largely of the first generation to have been born, raised, and schooled completely after the fall of the old regime in 1989. Having grown up with more freedom and been exposed to a wider variety of outside influences, the present generation of Czechs is likely to give the visitor a very different impression of Czech culture than its parents did.

Thanks to the improvement in language teaching in state schools, they tend to be more proficient in foreign languages and, as a result, much more confident when interacting with foreign visitors. Also, with greater opportunities to travel and the wide availability of foreign media, they are more receptive to and curious about other cultures. This is not to say that younger Czechs have abandoned the values of previous generations, but they certainly have set themselves apart in notable ways.

IGNORE THY NEIGHBOR

For visitors from close-knit societies with a strong sense of community, the lack of cohesiveness in Czech society may come as a bit of a shock.

Most Czechs will freely concede that they can be reserved, and most tend to value privacy. Many may have lived in the same building with the same neighbors for twenty years or more and yet still not have associated with them beyond exchanging greetings in the corridor.

This should not be taken to mean that Czechs are antisocial or that they won't be there for you if you should need help. Czech society is simply one that does not throw the word "friend" around carelessly. You do not need to look too far back into history to understand this aspect of the Czech psyche.

During the Socialist era, every facet of life in the former Czechoslovakia was overseen by the StB (Státní Bezpečnost), the secret police of the Socialist regime. The StB kept files on all citizens and offered attractive incentives to people who were willing to work as informers. Needless to say, the existence of such a body and the nature of its activities bred an environment of distrust and suspicion. You never knew who was on the StB payroll and therefore it didn't pay to have a particularly big circle of friends or to get to know your neighbors well.

If you had a neighbor who had piqued the interest of the StB, you could expect a visit from agents that would certainly be unpleasant. The StB had wide-ranging powers and were unscrupulous when it came to interrogating people. They had the power to harm the professional, educational, and housing prospects of individuals and entire families if they decided to do so. In the face of this, the best way to minimize the chances of the StB negatively affecting your life and that of your family was to know as little as possible about those living adjacent to you and to keep yourself to yourself. Despite the dissolution of the StB in 1990 and the sanctions brought against its members, it is testament to the lasting psychological effects of this institution that those who can remember life under it may still be reluctant to talk about it.

Czechs continue to be careful about whom they call a friend. However, this does come with the benefit of knowing that they are serious and sincere about it when they do call someone a friend.

ENVY AND WEALTH

As mentioned earlier, many Czechs maintain that envy is part of their national character. Where this notion comes from is debatable, with some saying it goes back to the sort of favoritism that came with good Party connections under the Socialist regime. With good connections, an entire level of privilege in many avenues of life would open up, which those with fewer or no connections could only dream of or resent.

Even if that were the case, however, it probably goes back further. Certainly the occupying German forces in the Second World War and, earlier, the overlords of the Habsburg Empire before the birth of the First Republic also found willing partners among the population who were prepared to trade loyalty to their country for personal gain by ingratiating themselves with those in power. Such is the darker side of human nature. Whatever the truth, it is typically those who remember the Socialist era who speak of envy. Many younger Czechs claim not to be affected by it in the same way.

Generally speaking, Czechs are not hung up on status symbols and consider it poor taste to brag about or flaunt one's wealth and possessions. In fact, some Czechs tend to downplay their wealth, regardless of how great it may actually be. This stems from the Czech liking for privacy.

ATTITUDES TOWARD IMMIGRANTS AND FOREIGNERS

More than a few publications have used the word "xenophobic" to describe the Czech attitude toward outsiders; often Czechs use it to describe themselves. However, even a quick look at the contemporary face of the country shows that, while there are certainly anti-immigrant sentiments in some quarters, to paint the entire nation as "xenophobic" is a gross overstatement.

Czechs can be a bit slow to warm to foreigners compared to some of their neighbors, but to construe this as a dislike of outsiders is to jump to the wrong conclusion. The Czech Republic has a strong tourism industry, many multinational companies have branches here, and with several universities in the country, foreign students and workers are part of the fabric of everyday life in the larger centers. These are not the marks of a "xenophobic" nation.

Additionally, according to the Czech Statistical Office, the number of foreigners living in the Czech Republic on long-term visas or with permanent residency has been steadily on the rise from 1993 to the present. In 2014, the Czech government struck down a law that had previously made it a daunting proposition for a foreigner to apply for Czech citizenship. The old law made very little allowance for one to hold dual or multiple citizenships alongside Czech citizenship, and required most applicants to provide proof they had surrendered all other citizenships as part of their Czech citizenship application.

In recent years, there has also been a rise in the number of agencies set up to help foreigners adapt to life in the Czech Republic and to navigate the bureaucratic machinery involved in becoming legal there. Czech society may not be as ethnically diverse as some of its neighbors, but it is certainly not "xenophobic."

SEXUAL ATTITUDES

Czech attitudes toward sex are not all that different from what you might find in other developed countries. From a sociological point of view, this could be considered a socially liberal society. Visitors from conservative backgrounds would probably regard it as sexually permissive. The Czechs are generally relaxed when it comes to subjects such as abortion, contraception,

LGBTQ people, and premarital sex, in marked contrast to their neighbor to the north, Poland.

Some publications also suggest that the Czechs have a higher tolerance of marital infidelity. This, however, is rather misleading, as a number of surveys have shown that most Czechs regard extramarital affairs as immoral, though they try to take a nonjudgmental stance toward those who have strayed. Perhaps it would be better to say that Czech society is more tolerant of human weakness in the face of temptation than it is of the act of marital infidelity itself.

Contraceptives are freely available in the Czech Republic, unlike in Poland where they are tightly regulated and where women face an uphill struggle getting their reproductive rights recognized by lawmakers. And in Poland attitudes toward the LGBTQ community are quite intolerant in the main: they have few legal rights compared to their Czech counterparts (see pages 62–3).

WOMEN IN CZECH SOCIETY

The role of women in Czech society, and Czech society's view of women, is currently in a state of change—slow change, but change nonetheless. Part of that change lies in differing generational values. Many younger Czech men, particularly in the cities, have divested themselves of a layer or two of *machismo* and taken greater interest in being part of home life than Czech men of even just a generation ago.

While older Czech men often wouldn't consider lifting a finger to help around the house, many of the younger generation share in the cooking, cleaning, or other household chores. The idea of paternity leave is slowly catching on in Czech society and an increasing number of young fathers can be seen out and about with babies in strollers and taking their youngsters to school.

The concept of feminism was a hard sell among Czech women for many years for a number of reasons, not least of which was that the supposedly progressive Socialist brand of "equality" existed in name only, causing generations of Czech women to take a skeptical view of the idea. Under the old regime, Czech women were able to study for and work in many of the same fields as men. However, they were still expected to fulfill all the usual expectations of women, such as getting married, having children, and running the home. Women came home exhausted from their "equal" jobs only to be faced with domestic duties. At the same time, men were not expected to contribute in any way to the running of the home. In the circumstances, it's not difficult to see why Czech women were so skeptical about the newer notions of feminism and equality.

A quick look at Czech history reveals another possible reason feminism took so long to catch on; Czech history had not forgotten the women who made a significant contribution to the development of national life. Important Czech women feature on the 500 and 2,000 koruna banknotes.

Just as many of the younger generation of Czech men are doing an about-face in regards to their place at home and in family life, many of the younger generation of Czech women take a more welcoming view of feminism than their mothers did. Czech women are waiting longer to get married and start families, if they choose to do either at all. Many put their professional development and education ahead of settling down into family life.

This is not to say that Czech women have it easy. They face many of the same obstacles that women in other societies do. In terms of employment and pay, Czech women still struggle to be taken seriously in certain fields.

Young women being interviewed for work typically also face the uncomfortable, and illegal, question of whether they are planning to start a family. Given the Czech Republic's generous maternity leave allowance and conditions, it is understandable why an employer might cross legal lines to ask such a question. Unfortunately, if the young woman wants a chance to get the job, she'll probably have to answer that question, regardless of her legal right not to.

As in many other countries, violence against women is a concern. In May 2016, the Czech Republic was a signatory to the Istanbul Convention, which was created to combat violence against women and domestic violence. As of late 2021, the Czech government had yet to ratify the convention.

However, Czech women are not helpless and certainly not without support. The Czech Women's Lobby, established in 2004, is a network of more than thirty NGOs around the country connected to women's issues at home and abroad.

There is a movement in the country to generate interest among women in STEM (Science, Technology, Engineering, and Mathematics) work fields. To that end, the award-winning Czechitas organization was established in 2014, to promote and maintain interest among girls and young women in learning computer programming and other skills essential in the IT sector. The Czech Women's Lobby and Czechitas are but two examples of initiatives being taken to improve the position of Czech women. Much work remains to be done, but positive things are surely happening.

THE ROMA

The Roma, or Gypsies, are the best-known ethnic minority in the Czech Republic and a group of people about whom many Czechs have very strong opinions. Generally characterized as work-shy nuisances and troublemakers, the Roma have been subjected to persecution since the medieval period in Europe.

Today, the rift between the Roma and the rest of Czech society is deep and the fall of Socialism has done little to help close it. A big part of this goes back to the Holocaust, when nearly all Czech Roma living in western Czechoslovakia were exterminated. In the wake of the Second World War, many Slovak Roma from the eastern part of the country migrated—or were forcibly relocated—to the west to work in heavy industry in the areas recently expropriated from the expelled ethnic German Sudeten Czechs. This created a situation where the Roma in postwar Czechoslovakia differed from both their Roma predecessors and their new Czech neighbors in mentality, typically identifying more with their Slovak background than wishing to adapt to Czech ways.

Socialism did the Roma absolutely no favors as it subjected them to systematic marginalization. This led to a significantly lower literacy rate among the Roma compared to other members of society, which sharply curtailed their educational opportunities. Roma children were typically ostracized and bullied in schools—that's if their parents sent them to school at all, which many didn't.

Under Socialism, the Roma were subjected to a number of abhorrent social programs, one of which included the forced sterilization of a number of Roma women. To this day, they have not received proper compensation.

The Roma communities still have some of the lowest literacy rates and highest unemployment rates in the country. There is still a strong antipathy toward them in wider Czech society, which in turn affects their educational, housing, and work opportunities.

There is also a rift among the Roma themselves, with many making an honest attempt to create a better face for the group while others seem content to sit back and "play the victim card," as the saying goes. In this situation, the use of the word "Roma" versus the word "Gypsy" can be very telling. "Roma" has a more official connotation, and is often seen as more respectable than "Gypsy."

What's in a Name?

A case in point is the following remark made to me by a young Roma woman several years ago: "I'm a Roma. I have a job I found for myself, I pay my taxes, and I'm interested in self-improvement. Gypsies don't do that."

While hers was only a single voice, her comment has stayed with me as one of the most succinct expressions of the distinction between the words "Roma" and "Gypsy" made by those within the group.

While there is much work to be done to close the gap between the Roma and the rest of Czech society, all is not bleak. Since the early 1990s, the Museum of Romani Culture in Brno has been doing a fantastic job of showcasing Roma history, from their ancestors' arrival in Europe from northern India in the fourteenth century up to the present.

LGBTQ IN CZECH SOCIETY

Year on year since the fall of Socialism, tolerance and acceptance of LGBTQ people in Czech society has been growing. While the debate on legislating for same-sex marriage is an ongoing one for the Czech government, a number of surveys and opinion polls show that more than three-quarters of Czechs support it. Other surveys show that the majority of Czechs would have no problem with a same-sex couple as neighbors.

According to a report published by the OECD in early 2019, comparing the development of acceptance of homosexuality in the 1981–2000 period to the 2001–2014 period, the Czech Republic sat just below the group average for LGBTQ tolerance in the latter time span. In terms of general acceptance of homosexuality, the Czech Republic occupied 22nd place among the group's 36 nations, well behind established leaders such as Iceland, Sweden, and the Netherlands. However, it came in well ahead of most of its former Socialist contemporaries.

The Czech Republic, particularly Prague, has a reputation as being one of the most accommodating and safe places for LGBTQ people among the former Socialist European countries and in central Europe in general. Many predict that it will be the first of the former Socialist states to legalize same-sex marriage.

Prague Pride, established in 2011, is the largest and longest-running LGBTQ pride parade among the former Socialist countries and is held every August. Another annual event is the Mezipatra LGBT film festival, established in 2000, which takes place in Brno, Prague, and other places around the country in November.

While all this is quite positive, it should be kept in mind that it has been a long and rough road to reach the present situation, and most of the work has been done only since the fall of Socialism.

Same-sex relationships were decriminalized in the former Czechoslovakia in 1962, well before many "Western" nations did so. However, it was not possible for LGBTQ people to live openly under Socialism without negative repercussions. The StB could use a person's sexual orientation to severely curtail their educational and employment prospects as well as their housing options. Wide-ranging, comprehensive anti-discrimination laws for LGBTQ people didn't come into force in the Czech Republic until 2009.

While the heart of the LGBTQ community is firmly in Prague, there are a number of advocacy and support organizations around the country. As in many places around the world, it is more difficult for LGBTQ people to find acceptance in rural areas than in cities.

Some maintain that it is an overstatement to call Czech society tolerant of LGBTQ people when, in their view, it's more a matter of Czech indifference. Whatever the case, this is social change in progress, and time will tell if clear tolerance of the LGBTQ community gains traction in other areas of the country.

NOSTALGIA

The year 2018 marked the centenary of the founding of Czechoslovakia. Throughout the year there were exhibitions and events around the country celebrating notable Czechs and Czech products, both historic and contemporary. Those events, in conjunction with a number of television documentaries, made clear that Czechs have a lot to be proud of and nostalgic about.

We've seen that many Czechs look back with pride to the First Republic—the period between the founding of

Czechoslovakia in 1918 and the signing of the Munich Agreement in 1938 and subsequent occupation of the country by German forces in 1939.

This was indeed a golden age for Czech society. The newly established country quickly and successfully reached out and connected to the rest of the world. It was a time of growth in the arts and industry, and Czechs today have taken a renewed interest in exploring that part of their history.

As so many Czech contributions to the world have been technical in nature, it should come as no surprise that the country has many technical museums and monuments, large and small, showcasing the products and innovations of both individual Czechs and Czech companies

Many Czechs are also fans of vintage automobiles and are proud to keep and display models of historic Czech brands such as Aero, Jawa, Praga, Škoda, Tatra, Velorex, and Zbrojovka in running condition.

NATIONAL PRIDE AND PATRIOTISM

It doesn't take long after arriving in the Czech Republic to notice that the national flag is not flown in many places. This does not mean that Czechs aren't a proud people, but more that their sense of national pride is a subtle one that is, for sound historical reasons, not deeply invested in displays of the flag or other symbols.

When walking through a Czech town or city you can see attached to the outside of many buildings, both commercial and residential, metal devices made of a pair of upward pointing tubes attached to a flat plate. These devices are flag holders and a remnant of the Socialist period; one tube was for the Czechoslovak flag and the other for the flag of the former Soviet Union.

On particular days of the year, such as May 1, people were obliged to display each flag in the holders on their building. If a holder didn't have flags in it on a specified day, or the flags displayed were not in good condition, there would be questions and negative repercussions for whoever was responsible for the holder.

Having been forced to display flags in the not-so-distant past, it's not so surprising that Czechs today are not happy flag wavers. A notable exception to this is international sporting events, when fans enthusiastically bring out the national colors for the occasion.

If Czech national pride is rooted anywhere, it is in the accomplishments of the people and the qualities of the land itself. If you were to ask a Czech what gave him, or her, a sense of national pride, the answer would probably contain a number of famous names and inventions or comments about how much there is to see and do in such a small country.

Many Czechs define their Central European identity as being the "best of both worlds," in that Czechs can be every bit as precise, pragmatic, and punctual as the Germans while still maintaining the Slavic flexibility for improvization. With a culture that is not fully "Western" and certainly not "Eastern," many Czechs also take some pride in the retention of the koruna as the national currency, seeing it as one of the last vestiges of their national sovereignty in the face of growing pressure to adopt the euro.

ŠVEJK VS. CIMRMAN

Written as a satire of the Habsburg Empire and set during the First World War, *The Good Soldier Švejk* is a novel in several volumes by Jaroslav Hašek. It is considered a classic of Czech literature and holds the distinction of being the most translated Czech literary work, having been translated into no fewer than sixty languages. Hašek died in 1923 and the tales of Švejk were completed by his friend, Karel Vaněk.

At the heart of the novels the eponymous Czech hero makes the various authority figures he encounters look idiotic and incompetent. Švejk himself comes across as something of a simpleton—seemingly a heavy drinker and a malingerer—though one is always left suspecting that it's all for show, given how often he is able to get the better of those in charge. He is the sort of character who leaves you wondering whether he is incredibly stupid or incredibly smart

In spite of the accolades the Švejk stories have garnered over the years and the fact that they remain required reading in school in the Czech Republic, it's not difficult to find Czechs, particularly younger ones, who freely admit to never having read them and to not really being able to connect with the character.

Švejk is most certainly a product of his time. Many consider him to be a better reflection of his creator

Švejk, drawn by Josef Lada, one of the founders of the Czech comic book tradition.

than of contemporary Czechs and their values. Indeed, a quick look at Jaroslav Hašek's Bohemian way of life, heavy drinking, and anarchist views, shows that he modelled Švejk very much on himself.

Many books on the Czech Republic refer to it as "a land of Švejks," though even a short stay in the country will reveal to the visitor that today's Czechs have little in common with the character.

That, of course, begs the question of which fictional Czech folk hero a foreigner should look to in order to understand the Czechs of today. For that, look no further than Jára Cimrman.

The character of Jára Cimrman was created in the late 1960s by Zdeněk Svěrák, Ladislav Smoljak, and

Jiří Šebánek. The stories of Cimrman take place in the late nineteeth and early twentieth centuries. While Švejk occupied his time satirizing and lampooning authority, Cimrman satirized nobody and rather reflected the more modest and educated aspects of the Czechs.

Cimrman is presented as a genius and polymath who would have been lost to history had it not been for the accidental rediscovery of his works in 1966. The life and exploits of the man were initially memorialized through radio and later a series of theatrical plays.

In contrast to Švejk, Cimrman was a Renaissance Man who was tireless in his pursuit of learning and the acquisition of new skills. While Švejk was a braggart who liked to talk about how he played the system, Cimrman reflects the more humble reality of modern Czechs. As accomplished as he was, he didn't blow his own horn.

Cimrman was well traveled and held a number of professional qualifications. He was also a resilient underdog, which is often how Czechs see themselves on the global stage, who was responsible for a number of inventions usually credited to others. As the story goes, Cimrman invented dynamite, but Alfred Nobel got to the patent office minutes before him to claim the invention for himself. This aspect of the Cimrman stories reflects the fact that there are many things that Czechs have given to the world that the world generally doesn't know are Czech in origin.

Perhaps the best illustration of how Jára Cimrman resonates with Czechs can be seen in the survey conducted by Czech Television in 2005 to determine who the public felt was "The Greatest Czech." Respondents overwhelmingly voted Cimrman into the top spot, and Czech Television responded by disqualifying him on the grounds that he was fictional. Despite the disqualification, it speaks volumes about the Czech sense of humor that they would vote for a fictional character over real historical figures in such a survey.

For many years it was thought that the humor of the Cimrman plays was so specifically Czech in nature that it would be untranslatable and incomprehensible to people from other cultures. However, since 2014 the Prague-based Cimrman English Theater has been disproving this assumption. The English-language theater group has been working closely with Zdeněk Svěrák's daughter to ensure that the translations of the plays are as faithful to the originals as possible. In 2017 it performed one of the plays on a tour of three American cities to great acclaim.

The Cimrman plays have often been cited as a good starting point for a foreigner to sample the Czech sense of humor. They have sometimes been described as "Kafka meets Monty Python."

RELIGION

At first glance, Czech society does not come across as being particularly devout. In fact, some have described it as an island of atheism surrounded by a sea of Catholicism; the visibly religious nature of the neighboring states does tend to push home the point that the Czechs go their own way on matters of faith.

However, just as with national pride, religion is one more aspect of their lives that Czechs simply don't wear on their sleeves.

In the main, Czechs are not dedicated churchgoers and use religious-based profanities quite casually in everyday speech. Yet while the prevailing secularism may have roots in the Hussite Wars of 1419–36 and Thirty Years' War of 1618–48, Czech society is not completely devoid of people of faith.

Generally speaking, religious observance among Czechs tends to become more visible the further east you go. Perhaps the most religiously observant area is in the northeast. During the Socialist era much of the northeast was heavily mined for coal and other resources, as well as being a center for steel manufacture and other heavy industries. Being inherently dangerous lines of work, these occupations bred a higher level of religious faith among the people of the region. In the post-Socialist period, most of the mines and factories were shut down, and the faith that people had turned to to help cope with the high risk of their jobs was now able to sustain many through the massive unemployment that followed.

According to a 2016 Pew Research Center survey, 72 percent of Czech respondents claimed no religious affiliation while 21 percent belonged to various Christian denominations, with Catholicism taking top spot. The remaining 7 percent were non-Christian minorities.

CHAPTER THREE

FESTIVALS &
TRADITIONS

Czechs enjoy a good celebration, and there are plenty of opportunities throughout the year to join them in both internationally observed holidays and national and regional events. Despite their less-than-religious nature, a number of traditional Christian holidays and observances, such as Christmas, Easter, and name days, feature prominently in the Czech calendar.

NEW YEAR'S

New Year's Eve, or Silvestr, is a public holiday. The Czech name commemorates the consecration of Sylvester I, who was Pope from 314 to 335 and who later became a saint. With the adoption of the Gregorian calendar in the late 1500s, his feast day fell on December 31. Despite its religious origins, Silvestr celebrations are mostly secular.

Many Czechs prefer to usher in the new year in a low-key manner. Typically, the cities and larger towns are all but deserted outside their centers through the New Year period as people choose to take the time off in cottages out in the country. Some go farther afield for a skiing weekend in the Czech mountains or abroad.

It is also typical to get together with friends on New Year's Eve in small social gatherings, where the conversation is accompanied by a variety of finger foods such as the ubiquitous Czech open-faced sandwiches (*chlebíčky*), leftover Christmas sweets, and a bottle or two of locally produced Bohemia Sekt sparkling wine.

Some people go overboard with fireworks to greet the new year with a bang. Fireworks are unregulated and easy to purchase in the Czech Republic, which leads to drunken revelers in the streets on New Year's Eve, setting off fireworks in unsafe and careless ways. Because of the distinct possibility of injury to the revelers and those around them, it is prudent to stay off the streets. If you've been invited to a New Year's social event, make sure that you get there before prime firework launching time and stay there for an hour or so after the fireworks end.

New Year's Day itself is generally spent relaxing. While many people may be nursing a hangover, there is also the idea that what you do on New Year's Day will determine how you'll spend the rest of the coming year. As such, housework is definitely off the agenda.

Some people make a point of eating round-shaped food on January 1—lentil-based dishes are common— as the roundness is reflective of coins and shows a hope for wealth in the coming year. Many Czechs consider it bad luck to eat chicken or any other bird on New Year's Day, as your luck might fly away.

EASTER

Good Friday and Easter Monday are state holidays in the Czech calendar. This is the time of year when the faithful are most visible, and observant. The week before Easter sees a mix of pagan, Christian, and non-religious traditions. There are Easter markets in many towns and cities, with stalls selling decorated eggs (*kraslice*) and specially braided switches of fresh willow branches (*pomlázka*).

The *pomlázka* are part of a rather peculiar tradition in which men and boys gently "whip" their female friends and relatives while reciting a rhyme. In exchange, the boys are given decorated eggs and sweets and the men a shot of alcohol. The custom is supposed to keep women and girls healthy and beautiful through the rest of the year. Although the tradition has been questioned by some outsiders and feminists, most Czechs regard it as harmless fun. However, some women admit to dreading the day because of overeager male relatives, and the practice is less popular than it used to be in urban areas.

Some say there is an opportunity for girls and women to get their revenge, however. The boys and men have to stop beating the womenfolk at midday, who then have the chance to pick up the whips and get some payback.

Sticking With Tradition

A young man who had been a bit overzealous when a boy relates: "I hit my sister too hard once when we were kids. After lunch she hit me back as hard as she could—with the handle of the whip! I had a lump on my head for a week and was always very careful at Easter after that."

I've only participated in the whipping tradition once. On Good Friday in 2005, my girlfriend came home with a *pomlázka* and a bag of sweets. She handed me the neatly braided switch and a scrap of paper with some Czech writing that was, to me, largely incomprehensible and told me to: "Beat me with this stick on Monday while reciting the poem on this paper and I'll give you these sweets." Naturally, I was floored, not to mention a bit suspicious of being set up for a joke. However, the look on her face told me this was serious business.

In points further east in the country, with prominent Slovak influence, the willow whip tradition is replaced by the act of throwing water at girls and women; often the water is ice cold or heavily perfumed.

On the Thursday before Easter, Maundy Thursday, pubs around the country serve green beer and meals with a higher-than-usual vegetable content. Traditionally, this is a meat-free day known as "Green Thursday." As green vegetables are not to everyone's

Easter Monday came and, whip in one hand, poem in the other, I set about gently "beating" her. After laughing at the atrocity I'd committed against the Czech language when reciting the poem, she handed me the sweets. There was a surreal quality to it all.

Then, in a further twist, she informed me that a female friend of ours was waiting for me to visit and do the same to her. As I made my way to her home, *pomlázka* and poem in hand—seeing a few other guys out there doing something similar—I decided that surrealism might be giving way to something more resembling fetishism.

I've since learned that the *pomlázka* today is typically the territory of nostalgic parents with little children, and I've met more than a few teenage boys and young men who don't participate in the activity at all.

taste, a very Czech way of ensuring there would be a green-colored consumable more to people's liking was the invention of green beer.

CHRISTMAS

The biggest holiday in the Czech calendar is Christmas, which formally extends from December 24 through 26.

The Christmas season kicks off much earlier, however, with Mikuláš (St. Nicholas' Eve) on December 5, the unofficial start date.

On Mikuláš the streets of towns and cities fill with groups of costumed figures: angels, devils, and St. Nicholases. The tradition is for groups of these three to visit people's homes to see the children of the household. All Czech children know that if they haven't been good the devil can take them away in a sack. The role of the angel is to protect them from the devil, while St. Nicholas elicits a song or poem from them and gives them a little present in return.

If you ask Czech adults about Mikuláš, many will admit that in their childhood December 5 was one of the most stressful days of the year. The "best" devils are remarkably frightening-looking, especially for small children—with blackened faces, wild wigs, horns, tails, and a sack with chains—and it is ingrained from an early age that the devil with his sack is more than ready to take naughty children down to hell.

It's safe to say that such notions don't play well in North America, but in the Czech Republic it's a much-anticipated way to kick off the Christmas celebrations. Several times outside observers and the foreign media have grossly misrepresented this tradition to the rest of the world—happy to show the devils terrifying children while barely showing the angel or the saint at all.

As Christmas draws closer other traditions get underway. The baking of Christmas cookies in vast numbers and varieties is required work in many families, and the family bakers start several weeks in advance to

Christmas market in Prague's Old Town Square, beneath the towering steeples of the Gothic Tyn Church.

craft the tiny masterpieces, many of which are designed to "age" in the weeks before Christmas. From crumbly almond crescents to intricately molded marzipan beehives, the cookies on offer in Czech households will delight and astound. Unfortunately for visitors, very few of the baked goods and only the most common varieties are sold in commercial stores—the handcrafting necessary doesn't lend itself to mass production. There is a good deal of business around Christmas for individuals who have the time, skills, and resources to do baking in large amounts. Many people will happily pay a friend who has the means and ability to do their holiday baking for them. Some small bakeries and confectioners also take advance orders for Christmas treats.

About a week before Christmas, evergreen tree stands and, confusingly for visitors, huge metal or plastic tanks appear in public squares and on busy street corners. The tanks are filled with live carp, the official Christmas dish of the Czech Republic. Buyers can choose to take their fish home live, where they will be kept in the bathtub until Christmas Eve, but the great majority have them "whacked" and processed there on the street. The entrails are never thrown away, as they create the basis for the soup that is the first course of the Christmas dinner. The carp itself is fried in batter and served traditionally with potato salad. Non-fish-eaters might be offered *kuřecí řízek* (breaded chicken breast prepared like Wiener schnitzel), or sometimes a special rolled sausage.

Carp may not seem the most obvious choice for a Christmas dish, but the popular theory is that it was a cheap enough "centerpiece" to be affordable for everyone, even peasants. Carp is also a traditional Christmas dish in parts of Poland and Germany. Carp farming has been very big business in the Czech Republic for centuries, particularly in the area around Třeboň in South Bohemia.

Czech families celebrate the gift-giving part of the holidays on December 24, which is also the traditional day for the big Christmas dinner. The Christmas tree is a part of the celebration, and it is put up no later than the morning of Christmas Eve. After Christmas dinner, a small bell is rung to signify that Ježíšek—the Czech equivalent of Santa Claus, whose name means "Little Jesus" but who is not a religious figure—has come and the children can go to the tree and open their presents. Unlike Santa Claus and other traditional Christmas gift bearers, there is no established image for Ježíšek.

Christmas is very much a private family holiday, and it is unlikely that a visitor new to the country would be invited to take part in the celebration. Still, visitors can involve themselves in the season by wandering through the markets that are set up in various cities, eating at a restaurant that offers Christmas carp (*kapr*), or attending a church service.

Christmas Eve, Christmas Day, and the day after Christmas (St. Stephen's Day) are state holidays, and most businesses and all government agencies are closed. Because of the three-day holiday at Christmas and the fact that January 1, New Year's Day, is a state holiday too, some companies simply don't bother to open between Christmas and New Year. Those that do open are likely to be manned by skeleton crews.

OTHER NATIONAL HOLIDAYS

While New Year's, Easter, and Christmas are the big three in the Czech calendar, there are seven other smaller state holidays that are observed. For many Czechs, these days have no deeper meaning than a pleasant day off from work or school. If a state holiday falls on a weekend, the adjacent Friday or Monday is not given as a substitute day off.

May 1—May Day

This is the traditional day of workers and equivalent to Labor Day. While it was a very big deal during Socialism, it's simply a day off work for most these days. In the modern context, it is seen as a holiday for lovers and a rite of spring where sweethearts kiss under a tree, preferably a cherry tree, though apple and birch are also acceptable.

May Day is immediately preceded by the traditional Pálení čarodějnic (Burning of the Witches) holiday on the evening of April 30. This festival has its roots in pagan tradition and is generally seen as the departing of winter and the welcoming of spring in a number of European countries. In non-Slavic European countries the equivalent is Walpurgis Night.

Traditionally April 30 was the night when evil forces and witchcraft were at their strongest, and people would gather together and burn the figure of a witch to protect themselves by keeping real witches at bay with the fire.

Pálení čarodějnic is not a state holiday and is mostly a social occasion that brings people together, in either

large communal events or smaller private ones, to
drink, socialize, and grill sausages over fires. The
proceedings reach a climax when an effigy of a witch is
burned on a large bonfire.

May 8—Liberation Day

This state holiday marks the end of the Second World
War and the liberation of Czechoslovakia by the
Allies, an occasion shared with many other European
countries. It is a day of wreath-laying ceremonies
around the country and the main military parade is
held in Prague.

Plzeň puts some extra effort into the event through
an annual festival in the days before the holiday, with
a reenactment of the liberation of the city by US
Army units under the command of General Patton.
The celebrations include a parade of restored historic
military vehicles with reenactors in period Allied
military uniforms.

July 5—Saints Cyril and Methodius Day

This day commemorates the bringing of Christianity
to Great Moravia by Saints Cyril and Methodius, the
creation of the first Slavic alphabet, and the translation
of the Bible and other texts into the old Slavonic
language.

Many religious people take the occasion to make a
pilgrimage to the basilica in the village of Velehrad, in
the southeast. Velehrad was the heart of Great Moravia,
where Cyril and Methodius did their work, and is the
most important pilgrimage site in the Czech Republic.

July 6—Jan Hus Day
Commemoration of the life and death of Jan Hus (see
Chapter 1, page 28).

September 28—Statehood Day/St. Wenceslas Day
A combination of a secular and spiritual holiday,
September 28 honors the nation's patron saint, Saint
Wenceslas, and his importance in ensuring the strength
of the Přemyslid Dynasty and laying the foundations of
the Czech state.

October 28—Independence Day
Commemoration of the founding of Czechoslovakia
in 1918.

November 2—All Souls' Day
While it is not a state holiday, many Czechs also observe
a sort of memorial day on November 2, formerly the Day
of the Dead (All Souls' Day) in the Church calendar. It no
longer has purely religious connotations, but people still
visit and tend the graves of loved ones, typically leaving
lit candles in special holders. Czech cemeteries tend to be
beautifully kept up throughout the year.

November 17—Freedom and Democracy Day
This day commemorates two protests against tyranny
by Czech students. The original protest, against German
occupation, occurred on November 17, 1939, in the wake
of the killing of a Czech student by German troops for
his act of protest against the occupation. More than 1,000
students who participated in that protest were sent to

concentration camps and the Germans shut down Czech higher education institutions for three years.

In 1989, fifty years to the day of the 1939 protest, Czech students rallied against tyranny once again—this time against the Socialist regime—and started the Velvet Revolution.

REGIONAL, SEASONAL, AND PERSONAL CELEBRATIONS

Outside the national state holidays are a number of festivals around the country that are more local in nature. Typically, they don't include any days off work and are geared to take place on weekends

Famous Battles

One example of a local tradition can be found in Brno, where the cathedral bells ring noon every day at 11:00 in the morning. This custom harks back to the Thirty Years' War of 1618–48. Brno was besieged by the Swedish army and, according to legend, the general commanding the Swedish forces agreed to abandon the siege if he was not able to take control of the city by noon on August 15, 1645. On that day, with the city's defenders vastly outnumbered and seemingly doomed to defeat, a quick-thinking monk rang noon on the cathedral bells an hour early. True to his word, the general raised the siege and Brno kept its freedom. The event is celebrated every August on Brno Day with a costumed recreation of daily life at the time and a reenactment of the siege.

Reenactment of the Napoleonic Battle of Znojmo and Suchohrdly in 1809.

Another historic battle that sees a popular reenactment every year is Napoleon's famous victory over the Russian and Austrian armies at Austerlitz in 1805. Every year at the end of November and beginning of December, the anniversary of the battle is marked with a variety of events in and around the town of Slavkov u Brna—known historically as Austerlitz—to the southeast of Brno. The heart of the event is the reenactment of the battle followed by a special worship at the monument to the fallen—known as Mohyla míru— near the village of Prace, which is between Slavkov and Brno. Archaeologists still regularly find human remains from the battle in the region, and sometimes the worship at the battle monument includes the interment of recently found human remains from the battle site in the monument's crypt.

Celebrating the Harvest

Vinobraní, or wine festivals, large and small are
popular events across the South Moravian wine
country through September and October, with the
festivals in Mikulov and Znojmo being the most
famous. Wine producers from across the region set up
stalls for wine tasting and purchasing, while others sell
meat and cheese to accompany the wine.

A very popular drink at wine festivals is called
burčák, or "young wine." Basically, it's wine that is still
in the fermentation stage and continues to ferment
while it's in you. Good *burčák* is light in color with a
bit of fizz and is quite refreshing to drink. However,
many have made the mistake of treating it like grape
juice and downing several cups, only to have it
come back and bite them with a nasty hangover the
following morning. There is also typically a lot of poor
quality or fake *burčák* on sale around wine festival
time and it's best only to buy it at an official festival
from a certified wine producer.

The wine festival season usually ends on St. Martin's
Day on November 11. This day traditionally marks
the first snow of the year and the tasting of the first
wines produced from that year's harvest. While not too
many places see the first snows as early as that, the day
does come with the following proverb that represents
the coming of snow—"*Martin přijíždí na bílém koni,*"
"Martin is coming on a white horse."

The day starts with the opening of new wines in
many places around the wine country at 11:00 a.m.
Wine that is officially certified for St. Martin's

festivities carries a red disk-shaped label with a depiction of the saint on a horse in white.

St. Martin's Day can be seen as akin to Thanksgiving as it involves a feast to celebrate a successful harvest. Typically, the feast features roast goose, though duck is also eaten. In the week leading up to the day, many restaurants offer special St. Martin's menus.

A Southeastern Specialty

Further east, in the Slovácko region bordering Slovakia, is the festival of Jízda králů, "the Ride of the Kings." This has been going on uninterrupted and largely unaltered since the early 1800s and has been on the UNESCO list of Intangible Cultural Heritage since 2011. It takes place during Pentecost and is closely associated with the village of Vlčnov, which hosts it

Horseman of the King's company during the Ride of the Kings.

annually. It is also held less frequently in the towns of Hluk and Kunovice and the village of Skoronice.

The event centers on a ceremonial procession of young men—typically from their mid-teens to mid-twenties—who parade through the town on horseback and on foot dressed in traditional folk costumes. In their midst rides the "King," a young boy aged between ten and fifteen in traditional girls' clothing holding a rose in his mouth. The "King" is surrounded by his attendants, also dressed in girls' clothing, who carry drawn swords to protect him. The rest of the participants wear male costumes and interact with the crowd by singing and collecting money or through witty banter. Later in the evening people come together for food, dancing, and socializing.

The tradition's origins are obscure. While it was strongly connected to the observances of Pentecost until after the Second World War, there is evidence to suggest it has pagan roots. Whatever its origins, today it is largely a communal social occasion.

School's Out!

A tradition that can be seen in cities in spring is Poslední Zvonění, the Last Ringing, celebrating the end of classes by high school students who are in the process of taking the school leaving exam known as the *Maturita*.

Poslední Zvonění takes place at the beginning of a week-long break the students are given between the written and oral parts of the exam. While the week off is intended for study at home, many classes prepare themed photo collages that are displayed in the windows of local shops, or take to the streets dressed in costumes to solicit a "donation" of pocket change from passers-by. While the groups of students typically make a lot of noise, most are quite polite about asking for a few coins to fund their school-leaving parties.

Most Czechs take this tradition in their stride and see it as a bit of harmless fun by students under a lot of pressure. However, some regard it as a nuisance and would happily see it go away.

Dancing Days

Another seasonal tradition associated with high school students is the winter ball. From October to December every year, it's not unusual to see very well-dressed Czech youths around towns and cities. This is part of the tradition of *taneční* (dancing).

Taneční has been an annual rite of passage for young Czechs since the 1830s and is considered a leftover from the days of the Austro–Hungarian Empire. It involves students taking a block of dancing lessons in preparation for two formal dance balls in November or December. It is also practiced in Slovakia, Poland, and some areas of Austria and Germany.

While not mandatory or free, this enduring tradition remains popular with young Czechs.

Birthdays and Name Days

Czech birthday traditions are much the same as elsewhere in Europe or North America. However, there are a few details to look out for.

The person celebrating the birthday is usually expected to provide the refreshments, which may seem strange to North Americans. If you are invited to a restaurant for a Czech person's birthday, for example, it is customary for the host to pay for the dinner, although it is appreciated if the guests bring flowers or some other gift. At the office, a person celebrating a birthday may bring in their own cake to share with the rest of the staff.

The scale and location of the celebration, if there is one at all, is at the discretion of the birthday boy or girl.

Name days *(svátky)* are a custom that can be confusing for visitors from countries that don't also observe them. In the Czech calendar, every day has a male and female name attached to it, which will be the name day of people with those names. Some florists display boards prominently with the names for the day on them, while some daily newspapers and Web sites will have the day's names posted somewhere as well.

Typically, name days are not a big deal. At most, a person might get a handshake and some well wishes from colleagues and perhaps a small gift—such as wine or flowers—from closer friends and family. There really aren't any fixed rules about what to do on someone's name day and many people don't do anything at all. Remember when giving flowers as a gift that the bouquet should have an odd number of flowers only. Even numbers are for funerary arrangements, not happy events.

CHAPTER FOUR

MAKING FRIENDS

For visitors to the Czech Republic who can only spend a few days in the country, the possibility of making friends with a Czech is remote. Visitors who have the privilege of staying a little longer—or interacting in a workplace— may find it easier. If getting to know ordinary Czechs is a goal of your visit, you will have to work a little harder than the average tourist, but the effort will be worth it.

As we've seen, Czechs do not use the word "friend" lightly. This may be a legacy of the Socialist past, when one never knew whom one could trust, but even Czechs young enough to not remember that period tend to take their time before calling someone a "friend." The upside of this is that once you have made a Czech friend, the chances of their being the fair-weather type are relatively low. They'll be the kind of person you can call up in the middle of the night to help in an emergency, the sort who will make sure you get home after you've had "one too many" in the pub.

Most Czechs make friends the same way people everywhere do—in their hometowns, schools, and universities, and through common interests. In general, making a friend in the workplace takes a little longer because of the formality that persists at work, but some do socialize with colleagues as well.

It is not uncommon for Czechs to maintain friendships over many years and despite changing circumstances, and many have friends from high school or even earlier who are still considered dear to them. Given the small size of the country, they are able to see their friends more frequently and with fewer logistical obstacles than might be the case elsewhere. Longstanding friendships are easier to maintain here.

Groups of friends socialize together, often traveling on weekends to someone's *chata* or going to restaurants. Once you have been accepted by a Czech or into a close group of Czechs as a friend, you will find warmth and wit—but breaking into that circle is far from easy, given the length and background of Czech relationships.

SMALL TALK AND CONVERSATION

Meeting ordinary Czechs who are out socializing—in a bar, restaurant, or club setting, for example—can be challenging, even given the phenomenon of the shared table in many establishments. It is not the custom to start conversations with strangers in the Czech Republic, although there are things you can do to make such encounters more likely.

As in most places, making contact with strangers will be easier if you are alone or in a small group. (Naturally, using common sense about this, particularly if you are a single woman traveling alone, is imperative.) Few things are more intimidating than a large group of people speaking a foreign language—especially at the decibel level common among North Americans—so if you're hoping to meet Czechs, keep the group small and the decibels down.

Learning a few phrases in Czech will be helpful. The Czechs are proud of their language and are happy and pleased when foreigners try to speak it. Asking for help with the language is generally a good way to start a conversation. They are keenly aware of the trials and tribulations of learning Czech and are often sympathetic toward foreigners trying to make a go of it.

Another good conversational gambit is to show that you have some knowledge of Czech contributions to the world beyond beer, NHL players, and Škoda cars. Czechs are very appreciative when foreigners display a more than superficial knowledge of their nation's many achievements. You're sure to see eyes light up if you mention that you know soft contact lenses were invented by a Czech—Dr. Otto Wichterle, to be precise.

If you should find yourself engaged in conversation with a Czech person or group of Czechs, you can expect the discussion to be wide-ranging and deep. Czechs tend to be well educated and highly literate and are generally not afraid to voice opinions about politics or religion that might be too controversial to bring up in your own country. Expressing your opinions is expected and welcomed but be prepared to be questioned closely about your views.

Most Czechs will want to know what you think of them, and especially how they compare to conditions and people in your home country. It is not unusual to be asked directly, "Why did you come to the Czech Republic and what do you think of the Czech people and country?" You may want to think about your reply in advance rather than trying to come up with things on the fly. Czechs often give a bit of consideration to their answers in conversation, so don't feel the need to give instant responses. Generally speaking, there aren't too many taboo subjects for Czechs. However, some topics need to be handled carefully.

In spite of an overall good image on the world stage, Václav Havel is not seen positively by all Czechs. While many have a high opinion of him, others regard him as the man who allowed the country's famous brands to be sold into foreign ownership—though it should be said that many of those historic Czech brands would have been consigned to the history books had they not been taken into foreign ownership during the rather precarious transition to democracy and a free-market economy in the early 1990s. Some people also feel that he overstayed his welcome in the office of president, and was a bit too given to moralizing. Be prepared for the possibility of some resentful looks and terse comments from some Czechs if you mention him.

It is also not very tactful to mention how much cheaper certain things may be in the Czech Republic than where you come from, though that is not as easy to do these days given the rise in the cost of living over the past decade or so.

Be careful about criticizing the country or aspects of the culture. While Czechs typically don't get offended easily and freely complain about what they see as shortcomings in their own country, it is poor form for a visitor to be overcritical. If you are in full culture shock mode after a particularly unpleasant encounter with a shop assistant, rant to a friend in an e-mail, not to the nice Czech person you met at a restaurant who has already taken a chance by talking to you.

FROM "VY" TO "TY"

It is important to understand how Czechs conduct their own social lives. Most North Americans will find the level of formality in standard social settings confusing or even intimidating, but it is vital to maintain that respectful distance or risk giving offense.

As in many other languages, Czech has a formal and informal "you" for addressing others—"*ty*" for children, animals, and close friends or family, and "*vy*" for pretty much everyone else. Understanding this distinction is important, perhaps more culturally than linguistically.

Here's an example: two elderly ladies have lived across the hall from each other in an apartment building for more than fifty years. They have watched as governments have fallen, children have grown up, and spouses have passed away. They see each other every day in the hall and at the mailboxes. How do they greet each other? Using the formal *vy* and their last names (for example, *Paní* [Mrs.] Novakova). Even though a level of intimacy exists between them, they do not consider themselves to be friends, just acquaintances. As such, the two ladies cannot switch to the informal *ty* without causing confusion and possibly offense.

The same is true in the workplace. Most colleagues who have worked together for years will almost always refer to each other using *vy* and last names. Younger workers or those who see each other socially outside work may use the informal *ty*, but it would be highly unusual for that informality to extend beyond a select few. (Further issues of hierarchy, names, and formality in the workplace are addressed on pages 170–71.)

Among young people—especially university-age students—the rules are more relaxed. Not many young Czechs would go clubbing with acquaintances and call them Mr. Janáček and Miss Vrbová on the dance floor!

Still, the safest course for visitors is to assume formality. Although you will be unlikely to use the Czech *vy* and *ty* in addressing people, use a last name with anyone to whom you are introduced, especially in an office setting, within the bounds of common sense. If someone introduces themselves simply as Jana, for example, you should feel free to use first names straight away. But the Czech person should make the call.

NAMES

While on the subject of "Jana," it is worth mentioning that many Czechs will assume that their actual Czech name is too difficult for an English speaker to decipher and so will Anglicize it. This could lead to a foreigner being introduced to a room full of Janes, Georges, and Peters. It is fine to ask them for the Czech version.

It may seem to you that there are only a handful of names in use in the Czech Republic because certain common ones crop up again and again. It is true that, compared to English, Czech has fewer names considered to be "acceptable." And parents must submit the names they are planning to give their children to a sort of "name police"—a government bureau—who determine whether they are suitable. This means that there are fewer Moon Units and Rainbows in the Czech Republic, and a lot more Petras, Jans, Zdeněks, and Pavlas. Czechs do not use middle names, so finding the right Radek Doležal in an Internet search can be a challenge.

Additionally, it is helpful to know that women's last names almost always end with a feminine suffix, such as –ová, in Czech. This comes from the Czech language having gender cases in which all nouns have masculine, feminine, or neuter forms. Female visitors might find their own names "Czechified"—for example, if you are Susan Johnson, you will likely be called Mrs. Johnsonová in a formal setting. Even foreign celebrities are given the –ová treatment when they are discussed in Czech—Emma Watsonová, Madeleine Albrightová, and Angela Merkelová, to name a few.

Ová and Out

Until recently women were required in most formal and legal situations to add the feminine suffix to their surnames, even though a growing number were refusing to do this in everyday contexts. Many Czech women married to foreign men chose not to do it, while foreign women living in the Czech Republic often made a point of not adding the suffix on the grounds that the convention was sexist. Some younger Czech women, too, chose not to use it for reasons ranging from simply making things easier for people not familiar with Czech to more feminist concerns. Linguists joined in the debate, arguing that sexism doesn't come into it and that Czech is not unique in having gender cases, which are an essential aspect of the grammar.

The issue came to a head in June 2021, when parliament approved a bill that would allow women in the Czech Republic to opt out of using the feminine suffix on their surnames in official documentation. In July 2021 President Zeman signed the bill into law, to come into force in 2022.

TO THE *HOSPODA*

The pub—*hospoda* in Czech—is often said to be the heart of Czech culture and that if you really want to get to know Czechs, the pub is the place to start. This should come as no surprise in a country that's been making beer since years had three numbers, and wine since Roman times, and even the smallest of towns and villages have at least one drinking establishment.

A long-standing stereotype of Czech pubs is that they are smoke-filled places where the air has a constant blue haze. Happily, since 2017 pubs, restaurants, and other

Na zdraví! Beer sampling in the brewery.

public spaces have been smoke free, and most pubs have designated smoking areas.

If you're in a pub with a group of Czechs, they may question you about your experiences of Czech beer. This is a bit of a test Czechs typically run on foreigners to determine if they are in need of help to get acquainted with "the good stuff." If you like beer, this is a great opportunity to get to know Czech beers beyond the big names. When toasting, "Cheers!" is *na zdraví* (literally "to health").

If you're a teetotaler, ask the locals if there is a coffee shop or teahouse where you might be able to have a quieter conversation.

In the east of the country, you may be invited to a wine bar, *vinotéka*, instead of a pub. South Moravia is the main wine-producing region, where wine competes with beer for popularity. The Moravians are as proud of their wines as other Czechs are of their beers.

If you're drinking beer in a pub in Moravia, between clinking glasses and taking a sip you are expected to gently touch the base of your glass on your coaster. This is a Moravian custom and not done in other areas of the country. It is also only done with beer.

One point of etiquette if you're a man accompanying a woman: men go through the door first when entering. This is typically explained by saying that there could be flying glasses and chairs, which the men should protect the women from. This applies mainly to pubs; it is happily "Ladies first" in cafés, restaurants, and wine bars.

If pubs and cafés aren't your style, there are clubs of all sorts, often with live music, in the major cities. Cocktail bars are not unusual, and sisha waterpipe bars enjoy popularity with many twenty- and thirty-year olds.

SOCIALIZING

Most rules about socializing in the "West" hold true in the Czech Republic. Keep away from controversial subjects such as politics, religion, or other touchy topics and don't be surprised if your Czech colleagues don't want to "talk shop" in their free time. When in doubt, let the Czechs lead the conversation. In social settings, it's good to keep eye contact during conversation. Czechs also like their personal space and are not keen on a lot of physical contact with people they don't know really well.

Czechs generally prefer to meet up in public places, so expect many trips to pubs or cafés with your Czech friends before they invite you into their homes or other more private places. This is as true for a first date as it is for simply hanging out with friends.

Typically, a meeting place will be agreed upon in advance—in Brno, for example, someone might say "Let's meet under the clock." Unless they tell you otherwise, they mean a well-known clock that hangs on a building near the public transit junction on Česká Street in the city center. Be punctual around Czechs, even in informal situations. If you fear you'll be late by more than ten minutes, call or text to let people know.

Map apps, like Google Maps and the homegrown Mapy.cz, are very popular here, and your companions may send you a link with the evening's destination marked on the map for you. Many people use map apps to make the decision about where to go for the evening.

DATING ETIQUETTE

While dating Web sites such as Tinder have become popular—they're certainly useful for finding someone with similar interests before committing to a date—they haven't taken over from more traditional ways of meeting up. The rule book for dating in Czech society is slim. One thing to keep in mind is that being a foreigner does not make you any kind of catch on the dating scene.

Show up on time and be well groomed. If you're a man and don't want to turn up empty-handed, a small gift is acceptable. If giving flowers, one is usually enough (roses or tulips are typical) but make sure to give an odd number. Remember, even numbers are for funerals only.

If you're a woman dating a Czech man, don't be surprised if he pays for the meal with vouchers. This is quite common. Vouchers are a perk of many jobs and he's just using that benefit. Conversely, if you're a man dating a Czech woman, don't be taken aback if she offers to pay her share of the bill—just don't ask her to if she doesn't make the offer. If you should find yourself in either of those situations, don't read too much into it. The Czechs know the value of money and are thrifty.

As we've seen, Czechs are fairly relaxed about sexual relations. If you believe firmly in not having sex before marriage, dating a Czech could be difficult for you. That's not to say you should expect sex on your first date, but the subject will certainly come up.

If dating here has a bottom line it is that you should be genuine and down to earth. Throwing money around will impress no one; nor will acting like a lothario or a diva.

VISITING A CZECH HOME

For a Czech to invite you into their home is a big deal. Such invitations are not given lightly, and you can consider yourself to have been elevated significantly in status as a friend. There are a few general points to remember when visiting a Czech home.

If you are given a specific time to arrive, be punctual. Good hospitality is important to Czechs and the chances are that your host will be preparing multiple dishes that may entail tricky timing. Even if a full meal is not planned, come with an appetite as there will be copious snacks and finger food. Also count on a fair amount of alcohol being offered. Don't worry if you don't drink; your hosts won't take offense if you decline politely.

Don't offer to bring any food to share. This could be seen as an insult to the host. That doesn't mean you should come empty-handed, however. It is good manners to bring flowers (again, not an even number), a bottle of wine, and possibly a box of chocolates. A bottle of whiskey or another imported hard liquor would be suitable for a man.

The Czechs are houseproud and it's important for them to have a clean and organized home—doubly so when guests are coming. The first thing a visitor to a Czech home will notice is that outside shoes are left at the entrance and there is typically a shelf of slippers of various sizes nearby. Wearing outside shoes in a Czech home is a *faux pas* to be avoided; to do so would be a show of disrespect to your hosts and their home. An attentive host will offer you a pair of slippers before you have even taken your shoes off.

Some say that the rule about taking shoes off inside the house has become more relaxed in recent years, and is more at the discretion of the host than a hard-and-fast social rule. However, being asked to take your shoes off is still something you should be prepared for when visiting a Czech home.

Reciprocation of the invitation is not expected but is always appreciated. As a visitor, your options will probably be more limited, but inviting someone out to a restaurant after they have entertained you at home would be entirely appropriate.

CHAPTER FIVE

AT HOME

As we've seen, the average tourist is unlikely to see the inside of a Czech home, and even the longer-term visitor may have to wait some time before doing so. For many Czechs, their home is their refuge from the outside world, and they are careful about whom they let into it.

Despite its role as a refuge, the Czech household has not been immune to social and economic changes. While many aspects of home life have stayed the same, others have changed quite a bit

HOUSING

Visit any sizable Czech city or town and you will see *where* many Czechs live—in *paneláky*, huge Communist-era apartment blocks built between the 1950s and mid 1990s, made of pre-stressed concrete panels.

Although times are changing and home ownership is high, the majority of Czechs still live in apartment buildings. Despite the Brutalist-style facades of many of

Panelák housing estate in Prague.

the *panelák* housing estates, reflecting their Communist-era origins, external appearances can be deceptive. Many of the buildings have been extensively refurbished and modernized, creating well-appointed, contemporary apartments within the harsh concrete exteriors. Several have also had exterior renovations, often including painting in bright, welcoming colors.

Most Czechs who live in *paneláks* own their own apartment. This is another aspect of living in the old Communist-era buildings that can be deceptive—as *paneláks* typically host a very mixed assortment of residents. There is no particular stigma in Czech society to owning an apartment and living your life in it.

The lack of good-quality affordable housing in the cities has been a growing problem for several years. According to a 2018 study by the international consultancy firm Deloitte, comparing housing costs across European countries, the Czech Republic had some of the least affordable housing in Europe. Part of the reason for this is that while the population has been growing through migration, most new building projects in the country have been institutional or commercial in nature, rather than residential. The shortage has caused many people in larger cities to move to smaller outlying towns and commute to work.

Other factors behind the Czech housing crunch include lengthy mortgage approval procedures and high property taxes relative to the cost of living. A number of people have chosen to leave city life and purchase land to build houses on. However, this comes with its own set of problems, including a lot of running around to various offices for building permits and other approvals. Owing to a shortage of skilled tradespeople, those who go down this road have to be willing to put in a lot of the construction work themselves. It can be a long time before trained professionals become available, and then the quality of their work may be questionable. They also tend to be very expensive.

For foreigners it can be a bit disorienting at first to hear a Czech describe their apartment or to make sense of a Czech real estate ad. Typically, an apartment will be described in the most basic of terms as "X+1." The value before the plus sign is the number of rooms for living purposes, and the 1 following the plus represents a kitchen separate from the other rooms. The bathroom is not generally included in the room count. If a Czech says "I live in a 3+1," you can imagine a living room and two bedrooms along with a separate kitchen. On the other hand, if they say they live in a "1+kk," it indicates a single room with a small kitchen area as part of it.

Most Czech homes have a "WC" (short for "water closet"), a room with the toilet separate from the bathroom. Typically, the WC and the bathroom are next to each other.

THE CZECH FAMILY

Czech families tend to be close-knit, with family members living within easy traveling distance of one another for most of their lives, often with the proverbial apron strings kept quite tight. The family is the core social unit in life, and Czechs will put their obligations to it ahead of anything else. This is reflected in the fact that many employers have sympathetic policies that support employees attending to family needs.

Czech law also reflects the importance of family in society as it provides generous maternity leave and benefits relative to many other countries. Female employees are generally entitled to twenty-eight weeks paid maternity leave at around 70 percent of their standard salary, starting six to eight weeks prior to the delivery date. After maternity leave concludes, parental leave begins. Parental leave can be taken as two, three, or four years during which time the woman's employer must keep her job open for her to return to if she wishes. Parental leave includes a monthly government allowance, the amount of which depends on how long the woman chooses to take time off work.

Since 2018, fathers in the Czech Republic have been legally entitled to a week's paid paternity leave. Prior to that, fathers had to take time out of their holiday allowance if they wanted to spend time with their newborn babies.

Generally, the role of fathers has become more visible over the last decade or two. It's not at all uncommon to see a young father pushing a baby carriage down the street or accompanying his children to or from school.

There is no real correlation in Czech society between strong family values and marriage. Since the fall of Socialism, the marriage rate has been declining steadily and many young couples choose cohabitation over marriage. Many couples who do eventually marry have already had their first child. In 2017, nearly half the babies in the Czech Republic were born out of wedlock. That said, 2019 saw a distinct uptick in the number of couples getting married. Whether that was a momentary spike or a change in the trend, only time will tell.

Czech families are generally small, consisting of the parents and a maximum of one or two children. Children are typically taught to be respectful of adults and to work hard in school. Czech parents are not shy about laying down the law when their kids misbehave or don't do well in school, and it's rare to see Czech children being rude to adults or behaving with a sense of entitlement.

Multigenerational households are common and extended family relations are very important. It's not unusual to see Czech families on holiday with grandparents or other extended family members.

In spite of these strong family values, Czech society is dealing with the same problems of an aging population and low birth rate as are found in many other developed nations. Among younger Czechs, this is down to rising living costs and placing their careers ahead of starting a family. Many young Czechs are waiting until their thirties to get married and start families—if they choose to do so at all.

The inverted population structure that is becoming visible as the population ages is hitting the Czech social security system hard, and the country faces difficult choices about immigration and social services.

CHANGING GENDER ROLES

While very accepting attitudes toward dual-income households have been the norm in Czech society since

Doing the laundry, Prague.

well before the fall of Socialism, gender roles around the home have been changing in the last couple of decades. This trend is most noticeable in urban areas and in areas of higher education. It's also a difference that can be seen between the generations.

According to recent surveys and studies on attitudes toward gender roles, Czechs generally do not see the equal sharing of household tasks as harmful to the power balance in a relationship. Some surveys even show that more than half oppose the traditional gender-driven division of labor around the home.

By and large, the younger generation of Czech men is less work-shy and more proactive around the home with regard to tasks such as cooking, childcare, laundry, and other traditionally female jobs than men of even one or two generations ago.

GROWING UP CZECH

Life for children growing up in the Czech Republic is not all that different from their peers in other developed countries. On any given day in a Czech city, you'll see youths hanging out after school or on the weekend with their friends at McDonald's, KFC, or another favored place of gathering, chatting with each other and texting their absent friends or parents on their smartphones.

Most of the rites of passage are the same as for adolescents elsewhere. The age of consent is fifteen, the legal age for consuming alcohol is eighteen, and

Children with their parents in class on the first day of school.

for driving cars is eighteen—though it is legal to ride motorcycles or scooters of up to 50 cc at fifteen.

The Czech education system is set up in such a way that all students get a similar primary education, though secondary education options differ significantly. Generally, Czech children enter preschool at around four years old and primary education lasts for nine years. Toward the end of their primary education, students need to choose which secondary education route they will take. There are four main options:

General Secondary School (*Gymnázium*)
Usually lasting about four years, this is the option most Czech students go for as it is academic in nature and specifically geared to university entrance.

Secondary Technical School (*Střední Odborná škola*)
This also lasts four years and grants a school-leaving certificate that will enable the graduate to move on

to univerity or other post-secondary institutions. However, unlike the *gymnázium*, it leans much more toward business in its approach.

Secondary Vocational School (*Střední Odborné Učiliště*)

This is a less popular secondary education option, with a focus on professional and practical training. Usually lasting from two to three years and finishing with a vocational certificate— *výuční list*—graduates of this option do not continue on to university.

Conservatory (*Konservatoř*)

Typically requiring an audition as part of the application process, this is the option for those whose goal is the performing arts. Studies at conservatories last from six to eight years and grant the graduates the school-leaving certificate required to continue into post-secondary level studies.

The *Maturita*

An important rite of passage for many young Czechs is the passing of the secondary school leaving test—the *Maturita*. This is a two-part exam given in April and May to many secondary school students to allow them to graduate and go on to university (provided they then pass the university entrance exams). The test consists of a state section and a section specific to the school giving the test. Students must conquer both the written and oral exams in several subjects to pass, and to do so is considered cause for celebration and honor.

As we've seen, part of the school-leaving celebrations is known as the Last Ringing—Poslední Zvonění—which symbolizes the very last school bell the students will hear. In the weeks leading up to the tests small groups of aspiring graduates will gather in high-traffic areas such as public transportation stops and squares to raise money for the parties that will be held on completion of the exams. Putting a few coins in the can will be appreciated—and students often have some candy or other small treats on hand to thank you for your contribution. Apart from the themed costumed groups on the street, another aspect of this rite of passage is the display of photos of graduating classes in the windows of shops that have agreed to make space for them.

Maturita is most commonly associated with *gymnázium* students, though some other secondary schools also include it.

PETS

Czechs are generally animal-friendly. However, you don't have to be in the country for very long to see that they are dog lovers. It's not at all unusual to find dog-friendly pubs and restaurants here; in fact, many have water dishes at the ready for canine guests. Dog-friendly workplaces are also becoming common, and dogs are quite welcome on public transportation as well.

The Czechs have given the world at least six domestic breeds:

The Bohemian Shepherd (*Chodský pes*)
This is a very old breed of herding dog that goes back
at least to the fourteenth century.

The Bohemian Spotted Dog (*Český strakatý pes*)
Developed in the 1950s as a laboratory animal—there
is little evidence that it was ever extensively used for its
intended purpose—this breed's good temperament
makes it a popular companion dog.

The Bohemian Wirehair Pointer (*Český fousek*)
A hunting breed dating back to the nineteenth century,
the *Český fousek* almost went extinct in the early twentieth
century. It is both an excellent hunting dog and a family
companion dog.

The Cesky Terrier (*Český teriér*)
Recognized as one of the rarest dog breeds in the world,
the Cesky Terrier was introduced in the late 1940s.

The Czechoslovak Wolfdog (*Československý vlčák*)
An eye catching breed due to its wolf-like appearance,
the *vlčák* was developed in the 1950s by crossbreeding
German Shepherds and Carpathian wolves, with the goal
of creating a dog suitable for police and military work.

The Prague Ratter (*Pražský Krysařík*)
A small breed that dates back to the eleventh century.
As the name suggests, it was originally bred for catching
rats in both rural and domestic settings. Today, it enjoys
popularity as a companion dog.

   Dogs are by no means the only animals Czechs
enjoy the company of. Cats, rabbits, and birds of
various types are popular as well.

LIVING GREEN

The Czechs do reasonably well when it comes to sorting their recyclable household waste, considering that organized recycling programs did not get off to a good start here and left many people skeptical about the idea. The poor start came about when it was found that the colored and clear glass that people were being told to put into separate containers was being lumped together in the end. Happily, the skepticism seems to have waned and it's common to see the color-coded recycling bins strategically placed around neigborhoods being well used. Unfortunately, the bins are not very well monitored and are often abused by people using them as convenient places to dump their non-recyclable waste.

While glass, paper, and plastic recycling is well established, electronics and bio waste collection have been a bit slower to catch on. Red electronic waste bins and brown bio waste bins are much less common than the yellow, blue, and green containers for the better established recyclables, but are becoming more visible.

Individuals and companies are taking a hard look at reducing single-use plastic items. Czechs can be seen as being ahead of the curve in one small regard when it comes to using plastics—having one's own reusable plastic or textile shopping bag has been a fixture of Czech life since well before the fall of Socialism. In fact, some older ladies will proudly tell you how they have shopping bags older than their adult children.

SHOPPING HABITS

While American-style shopping malls and "big box" stores have become a common sight in urban areas and enjoy popularity for their convenience, many of the ways that Czechs have always done their shopping are still very much alive.

In larger towns and cities, every neighborhood seems to have at least one or two convenience stores in the form of a *potraviny* for foodstuffs or a *drogerie* for household supplies and toiletries. These are very popular, and while many are branches of bigger chains, others are still independently owned.

The bakery *(pekárna)* and confectioner *(cukrárna)* have stood up well to stiff competition from fast food chains like McDonald's and KFC. However, the independently owned bakery is a rarity these days, having largely been replaced by chain bakeries.

Similarly, in spite of tourist-attracting coffee giants such as Costa and Starbucks staking their claims in the thriving Czech coffee culture, independent cafés of both bricks-and-mortar and mobile types have held their own admirably with local clientele.

Open-air vegetable markets are very common and popular around the country. Some, like the centuries-old Zelný trh market in Brno, are very well-established fixtures of their communities and frequented by people from all walks of life. Prague has many street markets both in the center and farther out. Three farmers' markets near the historic center are Náplavka, for fresh produce and baked goods as well as traditional crafts such as pottery; Heřmaňák, dedicated to reducing single-use packaging, where you bring your own reusable bags for your purchases; and Kubáň, which also encourages reusable bags.

With Internet penetration of the country standing at nearly 100 percent, Czechs have taken to online shopping like the proverbial ducks to water. This includes shopping for weekly groceries through the Tesco supermarket chain's online service or those of the homegrown online supermarket, rohlik.cz, and having them delivered directly to their homes.

When it comes to making purchases, cash and bank (that is, debit) cards are the preferred methods of payment. While credit cards have become more common and accepted in shops, many Czechs still don't have them and can be outright wary of them. Some still aren't clear on the difference between a credit and a bank card and use the terms interchangeably.

CZECH THRIFT

Czechs appreciate a bargain and are happy to shop around for a good deal. While the younger generations tend to be freer with their spending than their elders, who still remember life under Socialism, many of them have a spending savvy that you don't see in their counterparts in credit-card driven societies.

Some might say that Czech thrift has its roots in the economic stagnation of the Normalization era of the 1970s and early 1980s. More generally, the lack of resources and competent tradespeople during the Socialist era bred a level of self-reliance and a strong do-it-yourself ethos in Czechs that brought their inventiveness, resourcefulness, and problem-solving talents to the fore, and created the cultural mindset of the "Czech golden hands"—"*zlaté české ruce.*"

The establishment of well-stocked big-box hardware stores around the country and the continuing shortage of skilled tradespeople has kept Czech golden hands in a good state of readiness. Many Czechs, old and young, enjoy a good DIY project and it's not at all uncommon to hear people talk about how they spent the weekend building their computer, or about how much progress they've made on the new house they're building. They typically won't pass on the opportunity to mention how much money they've saved in the process.

However, a good number of Czechs—usually men with an old-school mindset and more pride in their abilities than is justifed—tend to overestimate their own DIY prowess and award themselves the golden hands accolade. Even to the inexperienced eye, it does not take long to see which Czechs truly have golden hands and which only think they do.

There are more contemporary factors that encourage Czech thriftiness. One of these is dual-quality food in supermarkets.

Dual-quality food is a big problem in the former Socialist countries of the European Union and there are many campaigns against it. Essentially it means that even though a food product may have identical packaging in two or more countries, if you take a close look at the ingredients you can see a distinct difference in the quality. This has led many Czechs who live close to the borders of Austria or Germany—both of which have better quality food in their supermarkets—to do their grocery shopping on the other side of the border to ensure better value for money.

Another aspect of Czech life where thrift is evident is in shopping for clothes. While Czechs will spend a lot on their public wardrobes, they tend to spend much less on their "home clothes"—often bought from the many ultra-cheap Vietnamese-run shops in pedestrian passages or more organized marketplaces.

While personally thrifty, the Czechs can be very giving and charitable. However, they are careful about how they give to charities. It's very unusual indeed to see Czechs giving money to people representing charities in the street; a notable exception to this is the well-established Světluška charity for the visually impaired, which has run annual public collection campaigns for many years.

Most Czechs prefer to make donations to charities by bank transfer. This is evidenced by the popularity of the Pomozte Dětem children's charity telethon that has taken place every Easter for years. The telethon sees Czech television and film stars working the telephones. During the run-up to the event, the charity's mascot of a chicken in a floatation ring is highly visible and instantly recognizable around the country.

Another Czech charity worthy of note is Kola pro Afriku—Bikes for Africa. This charity, founded in the northeastern city of Ostrava, collects and reconditions unwanted bicycles and gives them to schools in the Gambia to rent to the families of students who live too far away to walk to school every day. With a growing number of collection points across the country, this charity has benefits at home as well as abroad: many of the bicycles are reconditioned by homeless people and former prisoners before they are sent on to Africa.

During the Coronavirus pandemic, People in Need—a Czech-based NGO that operates in around thirty countries—was very active in ensuring that those most affected by the pandemic, but least able to access help, received assistance and supplies.

WORK–LIFE BALANCE

By and large, the Czechs do very well when it comes to striking a good work–life balance. This should come as no surprise in a culture where the pub is frequently considered to be central to the national identity and where labor laws guarantee four weeks paid vacation and many employers offer a fifth week as a perk.

If you have business to do in the country, don't try setting up any meetings on Friday afternoons, as a large number of Czechs will have already left their offices and started their weekends in earnest.

With a wealth of things to do year-round, both indoors and out, in a relatively small geographic area, the Czechs are spoiled for choice when it comes to weekend activities that are close to home, and many make the most of those choices at every opportunity.

CHAPTER SIX

TIME OUT

Czechs take their free time very seriously indeed. They manage to maintain a respectable balance between work and home life, often in the face of pressure to adopt foreign work practices by the growing number of multinational companies in the country. Work hours for most office-related jobs rarely stretch beyond forty hours per week—although that is changing somewhat as younger workers commit themselves more strongly to career advancement—and weekend or evening work is still uncommon.

LEISURE

Many Czechs spend their hours of leisure in ways that are familiar around the world—watching television, going to movies and concerts, visiting local attractions, and participating in sports and outdoor activities.

They are particularly passionate about outdoor pursuits. Whether skiing in the Krkonoše Mountains in winter, hiking or cycling on the multitude of trails that crisscross the country, swimming at outdoor pools, lakes, or reservoirs in summer, or picking mushrooms in the fall—Czechs can reliably be found enjoying their natural surroundings while getting some exercise.

And why wouldn't they go outside at every opportunity? For the relatively small size of the country there is a remarkable variety of landscapes and many national parks and other protected areas to enjoy.

In addition to its breathtaking beauty are the historic attractions of the country. The expansive and UNESCO-listed Lednice-Valtice area in the southeast is popular with both locals and tourists who come to enjoy the outdoors and historic sites. Appropriately nicknamed "The Garden of Europe," the area encompasses nearly 116 square miles (300 sq. km) and incorporates two chateaus and several smaller monuments. Created by the noble Lichtenstein family between the seventeenth and early twentieth centuries, it is one of the most extensively and carefully landscaped areas in Europe.

The best way to see the whole of the Lednice-Valtice area is to take, at the very least, a long weekend and explore it on foot or bicycle via the large number of trails that run through the site. Some people even do it on horseback.

Weekends Away

For a lot of Czechs, the weekend starts on Friday afternoon, with many already in their cars or on trains out of the city. Some will have put in an extra hour or two earlier in the week or come in early on the Friday in order to be able to leave their offices before the buildup of outbound traffic from the cities.

In spring and summer, many will set off for an active weekend's canoeing on one of the larger rivers or hiking in the mountains. In winter, they could be off to do some downhill skiing in the mountains, or cross-country skiing just about anywhere there's a place to do it. Others might simply be heading to their hometowns to catch up with family and friends.

The *Chata*

One thing that has not changed since 1989 is the Czechs' abiding affection for the *chata*, or *chalupa*—the weekend cottage. These range in sophistication from tiny lean-to shacks to year-round inhabitable second homes. The

Traditional wooden *chata*.

importance of the *chata* has influenced everything from the Czech love of, and skill in, gardening and DIY to the way workweeks are scheduled.

In the Communist era, weekend cottages represented the only way Czechs could own a small plot of land, and they used the opportunity to create largely homemade structures where the extended family could get together on weekends and for weeks at a time during the summer. Getting back to nature is very important to Czechs, especially for those living in big cities, in part because of the belief that fresh, country air is vital for health—not far-fetched, given the poor air quality in Prague and other urban and industrial centers. While industrial and brown coal air pollution have decreased markedly since 1989, air pollution from automobiles has risen dramatically. Many residents view their summer and weekend *chata* time as a chance for their lungs to refresh themselves after the long, often smoggy, urban winters.

Starting around the May holidays, Czechs fix up their makeshift trailers and begin to haul equipment and supplies to their weekend cottages. By the time school ends in June, the *chata* is set for the season, and families begin to extend their weekends into weeks.

Activities at the *chata* unsurprisingly revolve around family, with gardening, hiking, biking, and home improvement topping the list of things to do. Any visitor invited to a *chata* for the weekend should try to find out in advance if they can expect a "second home" or a "shack" experience. They can be equally enjoyable, but one might require more preparation on the part of the visitor. Ask if you will need to bring a sleeping bag or mat, and whether there is running water, to help figure out what is in store for you. No strangers to roughing it, Czechs do usually realize that visitors may expect something fancier than what is on offer, so many will try to lower your expectations even without being asked. Whatever kind of cottage is there, expect good company, garden-fresh produce, and clean air (possibly for the first time in weeks) when you head for the *chata*.

CZECH FOOD

Czech cuisine is not internationally well known, so many visitors have no idea what to expect. In the main, Czech food tends to be hearty, filling, and rich. Many of the ingredients are basic—pork, potatoes, cabbage—but the end result can be delicious. The national dish is probably the roast pork, dumplings, and sauerkraut platter called "*vepřo, knedlo, zelo*," but there are also other perennial favorites worth trying.

Svíčková na smetaně—or simply, *svíčková*—is succulent roast sirloin with a sweet cream sauce, served with *knedlíky* (bread dumplings, a Czech staple) and topped with a lemon slice, a dollop of whipped cream, and tart berries. *Svíčková*, like many Czech dishes, is time consuming to make, and it is a point of pride for most Czechs to be able to say there is a time-honored recipe for it in their family or that their mother or grandmother makes the definitive *svíčková*. Many Czechs who have mastered the dish guard their recipes and cooking methods jealously.

Clockwise: Goulash with sliced Karlovarsky dumplings; Zelnacka cabbage soup with sausages and vegetables; potato dumplings with plums and raspberries; fried cheese with french fries and lettuce.

Czech "*guláš*" (goulash) is typically looked down upon by fans of the Hungarian version—it definitely has far less kick—but is a staple of the Czech kitchen. Chunks of beef in a more or less spicy sauce with bread dumplings, *guláš* is a safe choice for most visitors.

Řízek is the Czech answer to Wiener schnitzel, the pounded, egg-dipped, and breaded cutlet for which Vienna is famous. The Czech version is somewhat smaller, generally made with pork or chicken meat, and is often served with *hranolky* (French fries) or boiled potatoes.

Smažený sýr—or simply, *smažák*— is a Czech culinary curiosity that leaves most outsiders wondering what it could possibly be when they hear the English translation "fried cheese." It's a simple, cheap, and widely available dish that consists of a piece of cheese dipped in egg and breaded before it is either pan fried or deep fried. Typically, it is made with a semi-hard cheese like Edam or some other type of cheese that softens but does not completely melt when heated. It's usually served with french fries or another type of potato-based side dish and *tatarka*—the Czech version of tartar sauce. A variation of this sees the Edam replaced with Hermelín—the Czech version of Camembert—and the tartar sauce replaced with cranberry sauce. *Smažák* is an acquired taste, but most foreigners take to it quite quickly.

Moravský vrabec is a dish that features marinated and roasted pork offcuts—usually taken from the shoulder or some other cut with higher fat content—and served with *knedlíky,* steamed cabbage, sauerkraut, or spinach. This dish is widely available, but varies from region to region. *Moravský vrabec,* as the name suggests, is the Moravian version. Other areas of the country typically call it "*vepřový vrabec*" (pork vrabec) in menus.

Tvarůžky cheese is a protected delicacy that comes from the small town of Loštice in the eastern part of the country. Every culture has at least one item in its culinary repertory to make foreigners nervous about; *tvarůžky* is that item for the Czechs. While one of the healthiest cheese varieties out there, *tvarůžky* is an acquired taste. Its robust flavor and sharpness are distinctive and enjoyable, but *tvarůžky's* signature quality is its pungent aroma that can make people recoil. In a spirit of fun, Czechs typically talk up—and often wildly overstate—the aroma to make uninitiated foreigners unneccesarily apprehensive about trying it. Many restaurants offer a variety of dishes based on *tvarůžky*—some also make it clear on their menus that they only serve it in the summer months and only on their outdoor dining terraces. Don't feel bad if you don't develop a taste for *tvarůžky*. Many Czechs themselves turn their noses up at it—pun fully intended.

Soup is much loved in Czech cuisine, with *bramboračka* (hearty, sometimes spicy, potato soup), *kulajda* (sour soup with dill and potatoes), and *česnečka* (garlic soup, said to cure anything from a simple hangover to demonic possession) serving as particular national favorites. Soup orders are likely to be accompanied by a basket of bread or *rohlík* (crusty, tube-shaped white bread rolls).

Common desserts include *jablečný závin* (apple strudel) and *palačinky* (crêpes), usually served with fruit or ice cream or both. Another typical Czech dessert is *ovocné kynuté knedlíky* (fruit-filled dumplings), usually served with whipped cream or a sprinkling of confectioner's sugar.

DINING OUT

Over the past decade or so the number and variety of dining options in the Czech Republic have multiplied, particularly in Prague and Brno. The choice goes well beyond traditional Czech cuisine, and there are restaurants offering vegetarian or vegan-friendly dishes.

Street café near the Charles Bridge, Prague.

Finding smoke-free places to eat and drink used to be a challenge, but, as we've seen, in 2017 a smoking ban in public spaces came into effect. Today, smoking is banned in all public indoor places, including restaurants, pubs, and public transit areas, among others. There are certain exceptions, such as for electronic cigarettes and shisha-type water pipes. Failure to observe this legislation can result in fines as high as 5,000 Czech crowns.

While finding a dining establishment that offers meat-free options other than fried cheese has become easier, and the law has stipulated that you can now expect to enjoy a meal in a Czech restaurant without an unrequested side order of tobacco smoke, some aspects of dining in a Czech restaurant have not changed.

If you are from a country where the waiters fall over themselves with insincere pleasantries in hopes of a bigger tip, then the typical Czech restaurant experience may come as a bit of a shock to the system.

Generally, the waiter or waitress will take your order, bring your food, and maybe come around once during your meal to make sure everything is OK. Beyond that, they will leave you to dine in peace until you tell them you're ready to pay. They certainly won't hover around your table and make small talk, or behave as if you're friends. Also, if you treat the serving staff in a Czech restaurant in an entitled and disrespectful way you can fully expect them to show their displeasure by adopting a more brusque attitude toward you.

If the menu you're given is not multilingual, ask if they have one in another language; English and German menus are not unusual in restaurants here.

Soups, salads, entrées, and side dishes are generally sold separately. You will almost certainly be prompted to choose a *příloha* (side dish), but don't think that it is included in the meal. It will appear separately on your bill.

Restaurants are required by law to present you with a formal bill printed from a cash register, so don't be afraid to ask for an *účet* (check). It is still sadly rather common for restaurant staff to take advantage of tourists by adding extra beers or unordered bread to the bill, for example, and you should not be diffident about insisting on a full accounting.

Separate bills are easily accommodated in most places, and a cashier (usually a member of the wait staff but not always) will visit your table to tally things up.

TIPPING
....

With regards to tipping, it's a pleasantly straightforward process of rounding up the bill to the next reasonable larger number. For example, if your bill was for 132 Crowns then tipping to 140 wouldn't be out of line. For a bill of 135 Crowns, rounding up to 150 would not be unusual. If you're more comfortable tipping by percentage, 10 to 15 percent is acceptable.

Tips are presented when paying the check by telling the waitperson how much you would like to pay, including the tip—not, crucially, how much you would like to get back. For example, if the check is 400 Crowns and you have a 1000 Crown note and would like to leave a 50 Crown tip, be sure to tell the waiter 450 Crowns, rather than ask for 550 change. Otherwise you will be giving an extremely generous, if unanticipated, tip. Don't leave tips on the table.

In a cab, tips are not expected, but it is customary to round up the fare.

You will generally be asked if you want to pay together (*dohromady)* or separately (*zvlášť).*

One more thing to keep in mind: wait staff will not bring the check to your table automatically. One of the nice things about dining in the Czech Republic (and in most of the rest of Europe) is that there is no pressure to finish quickly. A waiter may visit your table only once or twice in the course of your meal to get drink refills or dessert orders—but never to pressure you to vacate the space. If you want your check, ask for it by saying "*Zaplatíme, prosím*" ("We'll pay now, please.") or "*Účet, prosím*" ("Check, please.").

Many Czech restaurants feature daily or weekly lunch menus, usually advertised prominently outside. These are intended for working people who don't have a canteen *(jídelna)* in their offices, and it's quite common to see office workers taking advantage of lunch menus and paying with meal vouchers given to them as a perk by their employers. The lunch menus can be a very good deal indeed—it's not unusual to find places where you can get a bowl of soup and a hearty lunch for around 150 crowns or a bit more; that doesn't apply to the center of Prague, however. There's really no need to buy fast food when better can be found easily for less.

An increasingly popular way of eating lunch these days is to order it online and have it delivered to the office. Delivery services such as the Finland-based Wolt or the locally based Dáme Jídlo have contracts to deliver for many restaurants around the country.

The average Czech is likely to have only one "hot" meal a day, usually lunch. Breakfast is typically small, maybe just *rohlíky* and coffee or tea, perhaps with some yogurt—though oatmeal is gaining in popularity. (The concept of weekend brunch is also catching on.) Taking a short break in the mid-morning for a light snack *(svačina)*—often something sweet such as a pastry— and coffee is not uncommon. The evening meal is usually nothing more elaborate than some delicious Czech bread and cheese or cold cuts of meat.

Fresh fruits and vegetables are still not that common in restaurants (except when deep-fried or in a dessert), but excellent produce is available in season at local fruit and vegetable markets. While Czechs don't have as wide a year-round selection of fruits and vegetables as North Americans are used to, what they do have tastes much better because it's in season and relatively local. There's nothing to match a perfectly ripe Czech strawberry in May or June or a juicy peach or plum in August.

CULTURAL PURSUITS

The country has a vibrant cultural scene, especially in Prague and other urban areas, and the Czechs are spoiled for choice when it comes to museums, concerts, and theater. Prague has two national opera companies, several major orchestras, countless theaters and concert houses, and more museums and art galleries than could be seen in a year. Many of the cultural treasures are housed in buildings that are works of art in themselves.

With ten centuries of art, architecture, history, music, and literature behind it, Prague can offer something different for every visitor. There are guidebooks aplenty to the main attractions of this fascinating city, including Prague Castle (Pražský hrad) and St. Vitus' Cathedral high on the hill above the Little Quarter (Malá Strana), linked by the fourteenth-century Charles Bridge (Karlův most) to the beautifully preserved Old Town Square

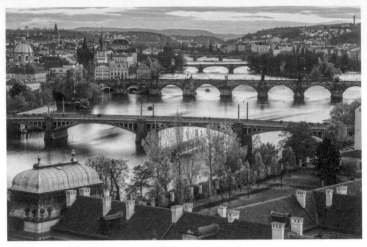
Bridges over the Vltava River, Prague. The Old Town is on the left.

(Staroměstské náměstí) and the ancient Jewish Quarter
on the right bank of the Vltava River; and to Wenceslas
Square (Václavské náměstí) and the New Town (Nové
Město).

While in Prague, you will not escape the lingering
presence of the legendary author, Franz Kafka. While
Kafka spoke German as his mother tongue, he was a
native of Prague and Czechs take him as one of their
own. Kafka was born in Prague's Old Town district and
spent most of his life there. You can visit his birthplace
and follow his life through many sites in the Old Town
before visiting his grave in the New Jewish Cemetery in
the Olšany district east of the historic center.

Certain cultural events in Prague are aimed primarily
at tourists, and you are unlikely to find any locals at
these. Concerts by "A Famous Orchestra" featuring
"Well-known Soloists" or performers in period dress
are strictly for tourist consumption. While these

The neo-Renaissance Rudolfinum concert hall and gallery, first opened in 1885.

performances may well be competent, keep in mind
that the city offers truly outstanding music and drama,
usually at a fraction of the price, in state-owned venues
such as the Národní divadlo (National Theater) or the
Rudolfinum (home of the Czech Philharmonic). Still,
for visitors in July and August, tourist concerts may be
the only way to take in some musical culture since many
national stages are dark during the summer months. In
any case, Czechs will likely be at their *chatas*.

Beyond Prague

Outside the capital there is an abundance of cultural
facilities of all types in virtually every corner of the land.
Many of the historic chateaus and castles that dot the
countryside also serve as galleries or venues for musical
performances.

The Czech Republic hosts many annual cultural
festivals on an international level. Easily the most famous

The opulent neo-Gothic Hluboká nad Vltavou castle in South Bohemia.

of these is the film festival in the spa town of Karlovy Vary. The Karlovy Vary International Film Festival has been going for more than fifty years, attracting an international audience and world-famous guests.

Music festivals of all sorts are also popular. The largest of these is the international, multigenre Colors of Ostrava festival, which has been held since 2002 in the northeastern city of Ostrava and has brought in some very big names to perform over the years.

Czech film is well known internationally and a number of Czech films and directors have done very well outside their homeland—some even winning Academy Awards—and, of course, the music of classical composers such as Dvořák and Smetana is famous worldwide. Czech popular music, however, remains a bit of a challenge for outsiders. This is largely because a command of the Czech language is pretty much essential to get anything from it. Most Czech popular musical acts perform in Czech and seem to have little, if any, desire to go international.

SCIENCE AND TECHNOLOGY MUSEUMS

Given the notable Czech contribution to engineering
and technology, it would be a shame to not take in some
of the museums that focus on those themes.

If you're in the center of Prague, a walk across Štefánik
bridge (Štefánikův most) and through the Letenské sady
park on the other side of the Vltava River will put you in
the vicinity of the National Technical Museum (Národní
technické muzeum) and its substantial collection that
covers a variety of technical disciplines and could take
you the better part of a day to see.

Right next door to the technical museum is the
National Museum of Agriculture (Národní zemědělské
muzeum), dedicated to some of the contributions
Czechs have made in farming, forestry, and other,
related fields.

If you're a fan of aviation, you should definitely
include a trip to the Letňany and Kbely districts on the
northeastern outskirts of the city. Here you will find the
world-class Kbely Aviation Museum (Letecké muzeum
Kbely) at the Kbely military airport. While the main part
of the aviation museum is at the military airport, don't
miss the smaller Stará Aerovka section of the museum a
short walk away on the Letňany airport property. Take
the red metro line all the way to the Letňany terminus
and you will be within about a twenty-minute walk of
the aviation museum. You could also take one of several
buses from the Letňany transit station to the museum.
The stop is a request stop called "Letecké muzeum."

FIGHTING FIT

In spite of the heavy nature of the Czech cuisine and the deeply ingrained pub culture—or perhaps because of them—the Czechs are, in the main, physically active and fit. In recent years an increasing number of companies have provided fitness rooms on-site for their employees to enjoy—or at least shower and changing rooms for those who like to run or cycle to work.

Many Czechs are avid runners, cyclists, skiers, hikers, or in-line skaters. Other popular sports include climbing, tennis, soccer, canoeing, and floorball. Swimming pools and gyms are available in most urban centers.

Walking in nature or parks is a less demanding activity that is also widely popular. In many instances, it's not even necessary to go far from home to do this. In the northwestern corner of Brno, for example, you'll find the city reservoir and the extensive recreational areas around it. On any given weekend during summer you'll see a good number of local residents exploring the trails that run through the woodlands surrounding the reservoir, either on foot or by bicycle. You'll also see a lot of watersports going on at the reservoir itself—swimming, kayaking, paddle boarding, and sailing are all popular activities there.

At the professional level, it goes without saying that the Czechs have been showing their world-class sporting prowess in many fields for generations. Young Czechs have never been without homegrown sporting heroes to look up to and to emulate, and Czech sports fans have never been without homegrown competitors to throw their support behind.

Sporting legend Jaromír Jágr.

The Czech Republic hosts top-level sporting events on a regular basis. It has world-class venues for ice hockey and figure skating as well as biathalon, cross-country skiing, equestrian sports, tennis, track and field, and motorsports. Many of those venues are available for public use as well.

That said, the country is facing the same battle with obesity that many developed nations are fighting. While you will certainly see a number of health-conscious Czechs making use of new technology and apps to track their athletic performance, much of that same technology has led to increasing levels of inactivity on the part of others. Of particular concern is the growing incidence of childhood obesity.

CHAPTER SEVEN

TRAVEL, HEALTH, & SAFETY

Getting into the Czech Republic is easy for most North Americans and Europeans. To enter the country—and the Schengen Area, which the Czech Republic joined in 2007—for stays of less than ninety days and that are not for business purposes, North Americans need only present a passport. It goes without saying that you should check with the Czech embassy or consulate in your country to see what the current regulations are— such things are changeable. Ensure that your passport is valid not only for the entire length of your stay in the Schengen Area, but also for a period of ninety days after you intend to leave it.

Most international flights arrive at Václav Havel Airport in Prague. There are also smaller international airports in Brno, Karlovy Vary, Ostrava, and Pardubice. Visitors can also fly to Bratislava or Vienna and make their way into the Czech Republic by coach, bus, or rail. Depending on your direction of travel, the major points of entry into the country by bus or rail are Brno, Ostrava, Plzeň, and Prague.

In the main, traveling around the Czech Republic is safe and easy, though the language barrier can be an issue once you venture outside the urban centers. The country has one of the densest intercity bus and rail networks in Europe. The public transit systems of many cities are integrated into the larger regional networks, so there are truly very few places that you would need a car to get to.

PUBLIC TRANSPORTATION

Public transportation in Czech cities is generally of a high standard, very affordable, and efficient. The Web sites of the public transportation systems of Brno, Olomouc, Ostrava, Pardubice, and Prague are all at least partly bilingual in Czech and English and not difficult to use. All public transportation stops show the schedules of the lines that serve them, and most larger stops will have easily visible electronic display boards showing when the next bus or streetcar is due and what line it's on. Additionally, some municipal public transportation systems have mobile apps to help you navigate the system better, and electronic tickets and passes. The Brno, Plzeň, and Prague public transportation systems all offer mobile apps.

Tickets for public transportation are affordable and typically interchangeable. In Prague, it's possible to ride buses, streetcars, the metro, and even the funicular at Petřín Hill with one ticket. In Brno, meanwhile, the same ticket that got you onto a bus, trolley, or streetcar can also be used for a trip on one of the boats that cruise the city's reservoir in the spring and summer months.

In most places around the country, one buys individual public transportation tickets at coin-operated ticket machines located at larger stops, dedicated public transportation ticket offices, or *Tabák* shops. It is also possible to buy tickets directly from the driver, but this is more expensive and requires exact change and the right Czech phrases to get the job done.

Tickets are available for different periods and transit zones, so it pays to check out the public transportation Web site to find out how long your journey will take and how many zones it will involve. Remember, your ticket is not valid until you've punched a time stamp on it using a validator machine when boarding the first vehicle at the start of your trip. Ticket inspectors *(revizor)* can be expected at any time so be sure always to have a valid ticket. The inspectors operate in plain clothes and are very good at their jobs—you probably won't realize they are there until they show you their badge and ask to see your ticket. If you don't have a valid ticket, you can expect to be escorted off the carriage at the next stop and be issued a ticket or obliged to pay an on-the-spot fine. If you don't speak Czech and end up dealing with an inspector who doesn't speak your language, don't expect the language barrier to get you out of a fine.

Increasingly, ticket vending machines that take contactless card payment are showing up in certain places. Contactless payment terminals are also becoming common on public transportation vehicles, so you can pay with your bank card when you board. The

Brno public transit system, for example, has the *Pípni a Jeď* ("Beep and Go") contactless payment system that allows you to pay with a card, smart phone, or smart watch as you enter the vehicle.

A very useful phrase to know on public transportation anywhere in the country is "*zastávka na znamení*" ("bus stop on request"). If you hear your stop announced followed by that phrase, find and push the nearest stop button to let the driver know you want to get off there. If you're standing at a stop and see "*na znamení*" anywhere on the stop's sign, it's a good idea to wave to the driver as you see the vehicle you want approaching to make sure they see you and stop. Some stops are "*na znamení*" only in certain windows of time. These will be shown on the sign according to the 24-hour clock.

TAXIS AND ALTERNATIVES

Czech taxi drivers, particularly in Prague, have a longstanding and often well-deserved reputation for dishonesty, despite many attempts to curb their activities. Taxis are required to have meters and GPS tracking systems these days, but these are not foolproof and many cabbies manage to find ways around them.

If you do not absolutely need to take a taxi, it's probably best to avoid them completely. If you find yourself in a situation where neither you nor the driver speak a common language, or the driver tries to haggle over the price before the trip starts, don't get into the cab. Generally, if you want to use a taxi in this country it is advisable to have a native Czech speaker with you to do the talking.

In recent years, taxi alternatives such as Bolt, Liftago, and Uber have found their way into the Czech market with varying degrees of success. In 2021, Uber was active only in Prague and Brno, while Liftago and Bolt operated extensively around the country. While many claim that such services are far preferable to taxis, it is safe to say that any precautions you might take when using traditional taxis apply to these alternatives as well.

If you need to go from the airport to your hotel or vice versa and have a lot of luggage, you might consider using a dedicated airport transfer service rather than a taxi. In Prague, there are several airport transfer companies with good reputations.

CAR RENTAL

If you are planning to visit cities exclusively during your stay in the Czech Republic, do not bother with a rental car. Parking is horrendous and Czech drivers can be aggressive—it is definitely not worth the hassle!

Many day trips can be done easily using long-distance public transportation such as trains or buses, but for some overnight stays or for places really off the beaten path, renting a car is a viable option. Many of the big international car rental companies operate in the Czech Republic, including Avis, Budget, Enterprise, Hertz, National, and Sixt.

The key differences between renting a car in
America and in the Czech Republic are car size—a
compact car in America will be bigger than its
European counterpart—and the rules car rental
companies operate under. Under EU law, rental
agencies must give you the full price in their quote.
By comparision, car rental agencies in America are
allowed to hit you with a lot of extra charges that can
add up quickly.

TRAINS AND BUSES

The state-run Czech Railways (České dráhy, or ČD)
operates efficiently and conveniently throughout the
country. There are very few places you can't get to with
one of their trains or a combination of train and bus.
In recent years, ČD has faced competition as the rail
business has been opened up to private rail companies
such as Leo Express and the Student Agency-owned
Regiojet rail service.

Tickets can be purchased without much hassle at
train and bus stations. However, it's just as easy, if not
easier, these days to buy your tickets online. The Web
sites of ČD, Leo Express, and Student Agency/Regiojet
are all multilingual and not difficult to navigate or book
through. Leo Express and Student Agency also operate
coach services in the Czech Republic and beyond—
in this, they have recently found a new competitor
with the arrival of FlixBus on the Czech market.
Additionally, all these agencies have mobile apps you

Railway bridge in the countryside near the village of Dolní Loučky.

can download to book through, check schedules, or
monitor the progress of the train or bus you intend to
travel on.

For the more adventurous, the IDOS Web site and
its associated mobile app offer ready, if not immediately
understandable, access to all train and bus schedules
at both local and national levels in Czech, English, or
German. IDOS takes a bit of time to get used to, but it's
popular and a great tool for planning your trip once you
figure it out.

Before embarking, try to find out where at your
destination the bus or train will deposit you. Even in
some tourist centers, the stations may not be centrally
located, so you'll want to have an idea of how to get to
the main attractions from the drop-off point.

WALKING, BIKES, SCOOTERS

The best way to get around cities and towns is often on foot. Prague's main attractions in the center are within walking distance of each other, and distances are much closer than they appear on maps. Bring supportive, comfortable walking shoes—the uneven cobblestone streets can be hard on feet and ankles. Outside Prague, most cities and small towns will have an easily walkable center, probably even a pedestrian zone.

The option of bike sharing is increasingly available in a number of Czech towns. A highly visible example of this are the bright pink bikes of the Rekola bike-sharing program, which operated in seven Czech cities in 2020. Another player on the bike-sharing scene is German-based Nextbike, present in ten Czech cities in 2021.

Several cities have also seen the arrival of electric scooters in recent years.

ACCESSIBILITY

For the mobility-impaired, the Czech Republic is no picnic. Stairs line the entrances to most older buildings, only few public transportation vehicles are wheelchair accessible, and uneven cobblestone streets can make getting around hazardous. A few metro stations in Prague and the larger ČD stations around the country have elevators, but overall it's a difficult country for wheelchair users or those with other special needs. Several nonprofit groups have been trying to pressure the

Czech government to improve accessibility around the country, but this hasn't been the priority that it should be. Happily, the design of many of the new buildings that have gone up in the last decade reflect a good deal more consideration for accessibility than the older ones.

Disabled visitors who ask will usually receive help from ordinary Czechs on the street, in terms of getting into and out of public transportation and navigating the city. Don't be afraid to ask for help (*pomoc*) as people really are used to assisting others.

ORIENTING YOURSELF

For most visitors to a Czech city, a general map with an enlarged inset of the city center will be sufficient for basic navigation. However, for those who want to get out of downtown or who have business in the country that requires travel to out-of-the-way places, the best resource is an Internet site called Mapy.cz and its associated mobile app. This homegrown equivalent to Google Maps is fairly self-explanatory: enter the name and number of the address you are looking for in the blank box (diacritics are not important) and choose the city you need to search in. The site will find the address on a scalable, printable map, and the map also lists nearby public transportation stops. The advantage of Mapy.cz is that the maps of the Czech Republic are usually more up to date there than on Google Maps.

If you're walking down a street in a Czech town and looking for a particular address, you may be confused by the sight of two numbers on most buildings. They'll generally be on different-colored metal plates—in Prague they are red and blue—but they will typically be in the same format wherever you go in the country, regardless of the plate colors. The upper number is the descriptive number with the name of the district (*číslo popisné* or *č. p.*) and is unique within each municipal part of a city and is issued by the land registry. The lower number is the orientational number (*číslo orientační* or *č. o.*) with the house number and the street name. It is unique for each street or square. For everyday navigation, the street name and the orientational number are what you need.

WHERE TO STAY

Star ratings on hotels and other forms of accommodation are not necessarily indicative of what you will find, since they are not closely regulated. Still, most accommodation options are likely to be serviceable and clean. However, they are no longer the bargain they once were, especially in Prague in high season. Expect to pay only slightly less for a hotel in Prague than you would in a major Western European city. Hostels are still a good deal for budget travelers, although they fill up quickly, and in the summer making reservations is not just recommended but mandatory.

Generally speaking, you can find just about any kind and class of accommodation in the Czech Republic.

Hotel Aurus in the center of Prague.

Hotels of all star ratings are available, as are traveler hostels and apartments. For the more adventurous, Airbnb and Couchsurfing are available as well.

However, if you want to do things the Czech way, seek out a bed and breakfast (*penzion*) for your stay. This can be a particularly charming and memorable experience when staying in a rural area. Just make sure there's no language barrier between you and your hosts before you book it.

If you're staying in a city and away from the center, the neighborhood you choose is much less important than its proximity to public transportation. Prices for downtown accommodation are typically higher than those in the suburbs, and if you find somewhere outside the center with good public transportation links, it can be just as convenient. When making a choice, though, be sure to ask how far it is to the nearest public transportation stop and whether you will have to use multiple forms of transportation to get to the center. Inexpensive lodgings may not be such a bargain if you have to ride an hour each way to get to the center. There is also the matter that regular public transportation will either stop completely at night or give way to a more limited night service, so make sure the night service—if there is any where you are—does go to a stop close to your address.

HEALTH

There is no special need for vaccinations or health concerns when traveling to the Czech Republic. Water from the faucet is almost always safe—although it may not taste great in some places—and the standard of medical care is high in terms of professional training and technology, though many Czechs themselves would say it needs work in the bedside manner department.

If you are planning on a lot of outdoor activities in rural areas, it is wise to invest in a vaccination against tick-borne encephalitis before setting off, or, at the very least, buy a good insect repellent specified against ticks (*klíště*) once you arrive in the country.

It is absolutely essential to have travel insurance if you are a non-EU citizen visiting the country for periods of up to ninety days. EU citizens are covered by reciprocal agreements. Always confirm with the Czech consulate or embassy in your country what the current health insurance requirements are—regulations can change. Also ask what is likely to be expected of you if you need medical care during your stay.

SECURITY

Changing Your Money . . .

One of the biggest risks that visitors have encountered here has been dishonest money changers. The center of Prague is notorious for them, though you'll find them wherever tourists or expats are present in large numbers. In early 2019, a law was put in place to give the victims of dishonest currency exchanges some redress, in that it gives a three-hour window of time for the victim to return to the point of exchange to have the transaction reversed. This three-hour period should be clearly stated on the receipt from the exchange bureau. While the overall effectiveness of the new law is yet to be seen, there is less and less reason to bother with money changers at all as time goes on.

The best and perhaps only recommended way to change your home currency into crowns is to withdraw them from an ATM (*bankomat* in Czech). ATMs are easily found in all arrival areas—the airport, train stations, and even border crossings—and offer visitors the prevailing exchange rate without any extra fees beyond that of the ATM company and the bank. It's a good idea to check with your home bank before you leave to find out what fees they charge for withdrawing money overseas and to make sure their ATM network is represented in the country.

If you must change currency, do it at an internationally reputable establishment or a bank. While they may not offer the best-looking rates, the fees are reasonable and there are no hidden catches, such as higher rates for smaller transactions. Never, ever change money on the street. To do so is not only illegal but also potentially dangerous—leaving you open to theft—and will likely leave you with worthless outdated currency that may not even be Czech.

Paying by credit card has become more common in the Czech Republic, but it's not as easy as in North America. Establishments accepting credit cards will have the familiar stickers on their front doors, but it is wise to ask before you buy or order anything to make sure that cards are accepted—Mastercard and Visa seem to have wider acceptance than American Express. Some places will also not offer their best "deal" to customers paying by card, as it requires both payment of a fee on their part and a record of the transaction for the tax police. It's also worth checking if your credit card company charges a foreign transaction fee—many charge as much as 2 to 3 percent of the transaction, and the fee is often buried in the fine print.

. . . And Keeping It

Unfortunately for Prague tourism officials—and indeed for legions of unlucky tourists—Prague has a not entirely undeserved reputation as a hotbed of petty crime. While there are very few neighborhoods in which it is dangerous to walk at night or where a visitor might be in actual physical danger, the chances of being robbed or pick-pocketed in broad daylight are not negligible.

There are some prime locations where such crimes take place—the metro and streetcars, crowded tourist spots such as Old Town Square, and busy restaurants—as well as perennial scams that seem to happen again and again. The gangs behind these thefts have made a virtual art form of their activities, and many people don't even realize they've been robbed until they reach for their wallet some time later.

Typically, the rustling newspaper or map distraction scam takes place on a crowded train and involves a team of three or four people. The first will cause a distraction, rustling a newspaper loudly enough to get your attention or confronting you with a map in their hand pretending to ask for directions. While they're doing that, the second person, behind you, will be lifting things from your purse or pockets, often slipping them to a third person who makes the getaway. There can sometimes be a fourth person tasked with blocking the view of the crime from onlookers.

Another common scam is a petition. Someone will approach you in a friendly manner with a clipboard in hand and ask you to sign it and make a donation. The "petition" will already have some signatures on it to lend it credibility. The signatures will be fake and your money will most certainly not be going to a worthy cause. Sometimes the scam can be used to cover a pickpocketing and the petitioner is simply a distraction.

It's not only visitors to Prague who are victims. Ordinary Czechs and long-time foreign residents are just as likely to fall prey to petty thieves. The best way to protect yourself is to be vigilant. A money belt worn under your clothes is the best way to carry cash, credit cards, and identity documentation. Once you've reached your hotel or hostel, ask about a safe for your valuables, and never carry your passport with you, unless you feel that your accommodation is unsafe. (Foreigners are required to have their passports with them, but a photocopy of the first page will suffice.) If you must carry a purse, make it one with a strap that you can attach to your body or to an item of furniture at any restaurant or café you might be in. Wallets should never be carried in back pockets—and even front pockets are not completely safe. Never leave valuables in coat pockets when you hang up your jacket in a restaurant or café.

If you should find yourself a victim of crime, you can report it to the police and may get some sympathy and an exotic-looking police report, but you are unlikely to recover your stolen possessions. You should find out from your credit card companies if a police report is required, however. The police department should provide a translation, although this may take a while. If you lose your passport,

City police station, Pisek.

be sure to go straight to your embassy or consulate as it can take time to gather the necessary documentation to have it replaced. Having a copy of your important documents in a separate location, or with a trusted friend or family member, can aid in this process.

Always be careful on public transportation no matter where you are in the country, especially during the weekday morning and afternoon rush hours. This is when streetcars are most crowded and pickpockets have their best opportunities. If you have a shoulder bag or rucksack, carry it in front of you and make sure all the zippers and other fasteners are done up.

CHAPTER EIGHT

BUSINESS BRIEFING

The Czech Republic is a business-friendly country with a diversified economy. Its major sectors include services, technology, research and development, manufacturing, and tourism. Czechs have a strong work ethic and qualities such as punctuality and organization count for a lot when doing business with them. Labor unions exist, but the majority of workers are not unionized or under any pressure to join a union.

While the business landscape and labor market have been subject to the influences of globalization, for foreigners who come to conduct business, it is increasingly important to do as much research into the company you'll be visiting and its corporate culture as you do about Czech business culture in general.

OLD AND NEW STYLES

Today's Czech business culture is a mixture of old-school ways, often rooted in historic Austrian and

Václav Pašek, former CEO of the Elektrarny Opatovice coal-fired power plant.

German practices, with contemporary, employee-friendly philosophies and trends that have become the norm in many developed nations in recent years. A series of reforms to the Czech Civil Code since the fall of Socialism have, to a significant degree, removed the business practices of that regime from the Czech business scene. Reforms that the European Union has been trying to put into place over the years have also had an influence on how certain aspects of business are conducted, not only in the Czech Republic but also in other EU countries.

While generational differences have a lot to do with whether a company in the Czech Republic takes an old-school or new-school approach to business, in many cases the sector the company operates in, as well as its age and the origins of its ownership, are also factors.

One of the rising generation of Czech e-commerce entrepreneurs.

Many sources of advice for doing business in the Czech Republic emphasize the importance of academic titles and the formal exchange of business cards, and both these things still apply. If you're dealing with younger people in contemporary fields such as IT, however, you may find them not quite as precious about their academic credentials. In fact, it's very likely they will have sent you an invitation to contact them on LinkedIn before you have a chance to meet them in person to exchange business cards. There's even the chance that they may not have business cards at all, if they work for a company that promotes the concept of the paperless office and reduction of waste.

Regardless of whether you are dealing with a company that takes an old-school or new-school approach, prepare yourself for generous helpings of bureaucracy both before you leave your homeland and after you arrive here. Be prepared to deal with hierarchical company structures—even companies that claim to have a flat organizational chart may still be more hierarchical than you might expect. Patience is definitely a quality you will need when doing business in the Czech Republic.

SETTING UP AND PREPARING FOR A MEETING

When planning a business trip to the Czech Republic, remember that there are definite times to avoid. Check the general holiday calendar (see Chapter 3) to make sure your visit doesn't clash with a Czech national holiday. Although many international offices are open on state holidays, work on such days is typically voluntary and many workers not only take the holiday off but also a few weekdays around it as well. The Christmas-to-New Year season in particular is a time of greatly reduced work—except for wrapping up the fiscal year, which ends on December 31—and is therefore a bad time for a business trip.

Scheduling a meeting any time after lunch on Friday is a nonstarter. Weekends start early in the Czech Republic, especially when the weather is nice, and many Czechs will prefer to spend their final hours of the week in the office by tying up loose ends or tending to tasks that require less effort and allow them to start psychologically winding down for the weekend. In fact, many will happily work a few hours longer on one of the other weekdays in order to be able to leave the office a couple of hours earlier on Friday afternoons.

In terms of time of day, you may find that your Czech colleagues want to start meetings at what may, in your culture, be an exceedingly early hour. Many Czechs start their workdays before 8:00 a.m. in order to be able to leave earlier in the afternoons, or at least have lighter workloads later in the day. Some claim that the Czech tendency to rise early is rooted in the Austro-Hungarian empire; because Emperor Franz Josef II suffered from insomnia and so started his business day at 6:00 a.m., the wider population had little choice but to follow suit. An early start to the workday is an old habit retained by many Czechs, though the influences of globalization and contemporary working practices have seen the ideas of

Listening to a speech during a webinar meeting of ISBNPA.

flexible working hours and working from home catch on and gain in popularity.

Two of the most important things to keep in mind when setting up and preparing for a meeting are always to have an appointment for your meeting, and always to be punctual.

Czech business culture is definitely not one where you can just "drop in" unannounced. Suggest a number of times and dates for the person you will be meeting with to choose from well in advance of the meeting.

While the Czechs don't have the same reputation for punctuality as the Germans, they certainly have an appreciation of it. If you're on your way to a meeting and it's clear you're going to be late by ten minutes or more— or perhaps late to the point of needing to reschedule— immediately contact the people you're having the meeting with. Unexplained lateness or absence does not go over well with most Czechs in any situation, business or otherwise.

Czechs, by and large, also appreciate preparedness; so things like a lot of disorganized paper shuffling or haphazardly put together PowerPoint presentations will lose you credibility points. Give yourself enough time to have a decent run-through of your presentation beforehand and to anticipate some of the questions you might be asked about it.

Don't be surprised if you're invited to meet virtually over the Internet via Skype, Zoom, or a similar program. You can apply the same guidelines to virtual meetings as you would a face-to-face meeting.

THE LANGUAGE BARRIER

In the three decades since Socialism ended, the Czechs have increased their proficiency in second languages to the point where the language barrier is not nearly as much of a consideration as it once was when doing business here. That is especially true of younger Czechs who have had many more—and better—opportunities to learn second languages than the generations before them.

Does that mean you should assume you can operate in your own language when you come to do business here? Not at all. While you may not need to hire an interpreter unless a lot of specialized jargon or legalese is involved, you will still need to agree on a common language with which both parties are comfortable.

English is a very popular second language for Czechs to study and many speak it fluently. French, German, Italian, and Spanish are also popular second languages. You may find that using Russian is an option. However, you should exercise some sensitivity about suggesting this as many older Czechs who grew up under Socialism remember Russian being forced upon them by that regime and may not be so keen to use it even if they can speak it fluently.

On the matter of translations, while going to the Czech Republic does not require much in the way of passports, visas, or inoculations for most people, it is worth asking well in advance about any customs regulations or attendant bureaucracy you may encounter, since navigating such seas takes considerable time. Depending on where you are from and the nature of your business, you may need to have some of your documents translated into Czech before you embark on your trip.

While you may be perfectly able to conduct your business in an-agreed upon common language with your Czech partners, learning a few basic phrases in Czech before you go will certainly be appreciated by your hosts. The Czechs are keenly aware of the difficulties of learning and speaking their own language, and genuinely appreciate any attempt by a foreigner to speak a few words or phrases of it.

INTRODUCTIONS

When it comes to introductions and greetings, Czechs are handshakers. A good firm handshake along with respectable eye contact when you introduce yourself for the first time—whether you are a man or woman—is quite important for getting off on the right foot with Czechs in any situation.

You should have printed business cards to hand, especially if you are in a position of some authority in your company or in the proceedings. While degrees and titles have lost some of their importance in Czech business culture, they still count for a lot the higher up you are in the company structure. If you have been given decision-making and signing-off authority, a business card with your professional titles clearly displayed will help establish your position.

Giving gifts is not expected in Czech business culture. If you come from a culture where this is done, keep the value of your gift to around 500 Czech crowns or less. A selection of promotional items with your company logo on them is sufficient if you want to bring a gift to your first meeting. Once you have built up familiarity with your Czech colleagues, Christmas cards or small seasonal gifts are, while not required, appreciated.

As for how to dress for a first meeting, this is where your research into the corporate culture of the company you're going to visit counts. Take the time to visit the company's Web site—their social media pages too if they have them—to get a feel for the atmosphere of their office and let that guide your decision on what to wear.

If you're in doubt, it's best to err on the site of caution and go in more formal wear—a suit and tie with good dress shoes for men and a blouse with a blazer and a skirt or dress trousers and nice shoes for women.

More generally, even if you can see that formal dress is not required, if you have a senior position in the company, do not dress completely informally. Business casual is the norm when it comes to clothes around the office.

Don't expect a lot of progress to be made at the first meeting. It will be more of a social event to break the ice and give everyone a chance to relax a bit and get to know each other. While there are exceptions, Czechs tend not to "get down to business" right away.

HIERARCHIES, TITLES, STATUS

Czech business culture, despite attempts by many companies to introduce flatter organizational structures, remains a quite deferential one. So figuring out who is "in charge" is generally not a problem.

Although many Czech companies claim to have stripped away their complex and rigid authority structures, hierarchy remains important. Most of the time the internal power structure of a company will be apparent; it is fairly safe to assume that the oldest male in the room is in charge unless you are told otherwise. Business cards (the number of titles, if you can't read the actual job title) can also be an important clue.

While observing the basic rules of deference to authority—shaking hands first with the boss, directing as much eye contact as possible to that person, not questioning his or her authority in front of subordinates—visiting businesspeople will need to gain the respect of their Czech counterparts. You will be at a disadvantage when it comes to proving your status if you are from a business culture that places little value on official professional titles. Making mention of your qualifications may be necessary to establish your credentials.

As we have noted, many Czech men who were children, or not yet born, when Socialism fell have a layer or two less *machismo* to them than their parents' generation and tend to be more supportive of women in the workplace and treating them as equals. As the younger generation—both men and women—rise to executive positions in Czech companies, women should have an increasingly easier time being taken seriously when doing business in the Czech Republic.

PRESENTATIONS

We have seen that Czechs appreciate preparedness and punctuality. Make sure to start and finish your presentation on time, know your material, and—if you have the opportunity—arrive at the presentation venue early to make sure any visual or technological aids you plan to use are working properly.

If, when giving a presentation to a group of Czechs, you find that they are simply sitting quietly and not asking questions, do not take this as a sign of lack of interest. They could, in fact, be very interested but are merely being courteous, deferring to you as the presenter and waiting for a convenient pause or until you have finished speaking before raising questions.

When the roles are reversed it's advisable to extend the same courtesy to a Czech presenter. This may be rather challenging if you come from a more confrontational and less deferential culture where interrupting someone mid-sentence to ask a question or challenge a point is the norm.

Also, if you are from an expressive culture where it is normal to talk loudly with a lot of dramatic body language and hand gestures, make a conscious effort to modify your behavior as Czechs do not generally warm to this style. Similarly, if you habitually use enthusiastic or encouraging comments such as "What a great question!" and the like, get out of that habit as many Czechs find this approach condescending and you stand a good chance of losing credibility if you use it.

NEGOTIATIONS

Negotiations can be a lengthy process and are sure to be frustrating if they are not entered into with the right attitude. Expect things to take time, and don't expect them to be conducted in an entirely straightforward manner. The hierarchical nature of Czech business culture can lead to delays as the person you are negotiating with may not be authorized to sign off on a deal, and you may have to wait for them to collect signatures from those who are.

Expect to do some haggling over the price, payment method, and currency before any road to a contract really starts to be paved in earnest. Don't be surprised if you're asked to do business in euros. While the Czech Republic does not use the euro as an official currency, many Czech businesspeople prefer to use it for international business transactions for simplicity.

Red tape and bureaucratic hurdles are inevitable, and the Czech Republic has more than its fair share of them in nearly every avenue of life. Efforts have been made over the years to reduce the burdens of Czech bureaucracy, but it's still a headache to navigate, for Czechs and foreigners alike. Quite often, it takes a fair amount of checking and double checking with various offices to find out what precisely is needed for a particular transaction.

On top of the local Czech bureaucracy, there may also be European Union red tape to contend with. This is particularly true for projects that get full or partial EU funding. If this is an aspect of the deal you're involved in, don't be surprised if your Czech counterparts openly speak ill of the extra paperwork and make some offhand sarcastic remarks about the EU making life more difficult for no other reason than because it can.

It is important to delineate clearly the responsibilities and expectations of each party. Tasks should be assigned to specific people, and the safest bet is to circulate a list of agreed-upon responsibilities to everyone involved shortly after concluding negotiations.

Any extra time and care taken in negotiating a contract here should be regarded as time well spent. Getting things right the first time round reduces the chances of bureaucratic hold-ups further down the line, with the attendant legwork of running around various departmental offices all over again. Your Czech counterparts and colleagues will certainly be thankful and relieved if you do.

CONTRACTS

Contracts are very important in the Czech Republic. There needs to be a contract in place for any transaction with a Czech company, and you should expect those contracts to be long and detailed, and to require a good deal of time to hammer out.

The Czech Republic is party to the United Nations Convention on Contracts for the International Sale of Goods (CISG). Consequently, international business contracts with Czech companies are governed by its provisions rather than Czech domestic law. CISG does, however, give a wide degree of flexibility in the drafting and adjustment of contracts.

Even if you are able to conduct negotiations without an interpreter, you will need a translator for the contract, which, for legal reasons, should be written in both Czech and your language. It is important to establish which of the languages used has legal standing. Sometimes both a Czech and an English-language contract will be produced, but the Czech version may override the English one legally. Clearly this is not ideal and, if at all possible, you should insist on an independent expert to read and compare the contracts, or else ask for an English contract only.

Once the work of hammering out a contract has been done, there will be a lot of signing to do. On the Czech side of the transaction you may see a degree of ceremony, as those who have signing authority will most likely not only be signing the agreement, but also putting their official signatory stamp with their signature. This is an aspect of Czech business culture that harks back to the time when a person's professional and academic titles were very important.

You can fully expect at least one notary stamp to be required somewhere in the process when dealing with any sort of officialdom. Notaries are everywhere in the country and people can make their entire living being one here. Keeping original, signed, stamped copies of any contracts is crucial. Czechs typically do not recognize photocopies, unless they have been notarized, and sometimes not even then.

Stamp-Happy

The Czech love of rubber stamps forms the basis of one of the most famous scenes in Czech cinema. Jiří Menzel's 1966 New Wave masterpiece, *Closely Watched Trains*—based on the Bohumil Hrabal novel of the same name—won the 1967 Academy Award for Best Foreign Film and includes an unusual stamping scene, to say the least. One of the main characters, a libidinous middle-aged train dispatcher, uses official railway stamps to seduce a comely young telegraph operator, stamping her legs and backside over and over until she can't restrain herself any longer.

SETTLING DISAGREEMENTS

Just as the Czech Republic is party to CISG for international contracts, it is also a signatory to other international agreements on arbitration, which can overrule Czech national law when it comes to dealing with breaches of contract. If Czech law has been agreed upon for the contract, however, arbitration may be preferable to drawn-out litigation. Czech courts have a reputation for taking a long time before they hear a case, and a long time once the case is underway.

Should disagreements arise in the course of negotiations, it is always best to try to solve them one-on-one outside the meeting, particularly if they involve a dispute that could challenge the authority of the boss. Given the Czech hierarchy in business, a direct confrontation in front of subordinates or colleagues could be so offensive as to derail the entire process.

If you are a foreign manager with authority over Czech workers, how you resolve conflicts in the work place may be affected by any specific protocols your company has for dealing with such situations, or if the staff are unionized. From a psychological standpoint, reprimanding an employee in front of their colleagues is definitely a no-no if you want to keep the respect of your subordinates. Whether you have to reprimand an employee or resolve a conflict between multiple employees, it should be handled in private.

JOB SATISFACTION

Many Czechs, particularly those of the old school, are reluctant to take on responsibility if they can pass it on to someone else, or they may not see a project in any larger context, only in terms of their own contribution to it. Essentially, they take an "It's just a job," or "I just work here," attitude.

It is less difficult to instil a sense of job satisfaction in younger workers in companies with modern attitudes toward management and employee motivation. However, the very low unemployment rate in the country makes many employers think twice before deciding to dismiss staff who are performing poorly, as it is not so easy to replace them. This has, in turn, created situations where younger Czech workers with poor motivation are sometimes kept on by companies and need to be watched closely. In either case, it's best that everyone involved in a project has their role clearly defined, in writing, before work even begins.

SOCIALIZING AND WORK

We have seen that Czechs, by and large, have a healthy and well-developed work–life balance. Business and pleasure typically don't go hand in hand here.

Your Czech colleagues will probably invite you to lunch at least once. This will be a social event to take a break from work—the "working lunch" is generally not done by the Czechs—and to enjoy the meal. It's a near certainty that wherever they take you beer will be an option, and they will probably have a drink with their meal. Just keep in mind that going back to work while clearly under the influence is as unacceptable here as it is elsewhere. If you're new to Czech beer or don't hold your alcohol well, you may want to order only a small beer or something non-alcoholic at lunchtime.

If such social opportunities don't present themselves, it's best not to force the situation. Most Czechs are proud of their country, and some even like to show foreigners around after business hours, but these interactions should be initiated by your Czech colleagues. Work is not nearly as all-consuming for Czechs as it is in some other cultures—the motto is more "Work to Live" than "Live to Work"—and some people can be quite strict about keeping work and home life separate.

CHAPTER NINE

COMMUNICATING

THE CZECH LANGUAGE

Czech is a difficult Slavic language with an intimidating set of diacritics, more consonants than look possible in one word, and a complex grammatical structure that features seven declensions, among other hoops to jump through. It may take several days to even start to recognize common words because of how hard the language appears to be to pronounce, even though it is written in Latin script. It will take much longer to figure out the noun cases and other grammatical peculiarities.

Czech is completely phonetic—once the basic sounds are learned, reading words and recognizing place names (such as on public transportation) becomes easier. The *háček* (the small "v" hook above certain letters) and *čárka* (accent mark over certain vowels) were actually introduced as an attempt to simplify spelling by reducing the number of diphthongs. Without the *háčky* and *čárky* diacritics, Czech would have many much longer words. From that standpoint, the diacritics are a blessing.

Image from the Old Czech Bible of Olomouc, 1417.

In the case of "*š*," "*č*," and "*ž*," pronunciations are relatively easy for an English-speaker. The sounds are pronounced as if the letter were "sh," "ch," and "zh." A *háček* over an "e" indicates a "ye" sound. The near impenetrable "*ř*" is unique to Czech and has a reputation of being the most difficult letter of the Czech alphabet for foreigners and native Czechs alike to pronounce correctly. It starts as a rolled "r" sound but ends as a "zh" sound—an English speaker will probably approximate it by rolling a sort of "rzh." There are even some Czechs for whom this sound is a problem, so don't feel bad if you can't master it. Vowels with *čárky* will be a beat longer in duration than those without, but most non-Czech speakers will not notice the difference.

The letters "*ď*," "*ť*," and "*ň*" present a further challenge. The diacritics on them represent a slight but perceptible "ye" on the end of the main letter sound. English has no real equivalent.

It's worth noting here that speech therapy is a popular and lucrative profession in the Czech Republic. This is because, in order to start school, Czech children must be able to pass a test showing that they can properly form key sounds required for speaking the Czech language correctly. A number of sessions with a speech therapist is often necessary to get some children to the point of readiness for the test.

No one expects foreigners to learn Czech just for a short trip, but visitors' attempts to speak the Czech language will be met warmly. It will go a long way toward creating goodwill if you observe a few "rules" about when to offer greetings and other niceties.

When entering a shop, approaching a market stand, or having first contact with someone, it is customary to say *Dobrý den* (good day/hello). Of course, it is also possible to use good morning, good evening, and good night, but the timing is tricky and it means memorizing more phrases. *Dobrý den* works pretty well all day. When leaving, always bid the person good-bye (*na shledanou*). A "thank you" (*děkuji*) is never out of place either.

On public transportation, conditions can be crowded and contact inevitable. Using *promiňte* (excuse me) will smooth the situation. Even *pardon*, pronounced with a long "o" sound and stress on the second syllable, is better than nothing. If you want to find out if someone speaks English, it's best not to launch into the question without first saying *Dobrý den*. Greetings are very important in the Czech Republic, even among strangers.

SURVIVAL CZECH

English	Czech	Pronunciation
Thank you	*Děkuji*	DYEH-koo-yee
Thanks (very informal)	*Díky*	DEE-kee
Please	*Prosím*	PROH-seem
Hello/good day	*Dobrý den!*	DOH-bree den
Good-bye	*Na shledanou*	NAH-shle-dah-noh
Do you speak English?	*Mluvíte anglický*	MLOO-vee-teh ANG-lits-ki
Excuse me/ pardon me	*Promiňte*	PROH-min-teh
We'll pay, please	*Zaplatíme, prosím*	ZAH-plah-tee-meh, PROH-seem
Cheers! (to your health)	*Na zdraví*	NAH-zdra-vee

OTHER LANGUAGES

Linguistic flexibility has been steadily growing among Czechs and it's not so difficult to find people who speak English or another language in Prague and the larger urban centers. Most service workers in the centers will speak at least some English and many young Czechs speak it quite well, but German may serve you better when communicating with older people.

Russian is also spoken by a large number of people as it was imposed during the Communist era, but many older Czechs are reluctant to speak it and may even become a bit hostile if asked to. Unless it is a very important situation, Russian is best suggested with some care and sensitivity. That said, however, in the years since Socialism a good number of younger Czechs have taken to studying Russian as a second language. So if the only second language you have is Russian, you may be able to find a younger Czech willing and able to speak it with you even if the older ones won't. There are also areas with large Russian populations—such as the spa town of Karlovy Vary—where Russian is certainly heard.

Communicating in situations in which no mutual language can be found is pretty universal. Armed with a phrase book, map, and small notebook—or the digital equivalents—it should be possible to get a point across. If the situation is critical, fall back on asking for an English speaker. Usually someone can be found.

BODY LANGUAGE AND PERSONAL SPACE

Czechs are restrained in their body language but still manage to convey some things without words. Never shy about disapproving glances, they are experts at the glower when faced with overly loud or otherwise unruly people, especially on public transportation. Conversely, if you offer your seat to an elderly person, pregnant woman, or someone with small children (as is customary and expected on public transportation), you are likely to be rewarded with a grateful smile. Failure to do so can put you back into indignant-glare land.

One Czech habit that many visitors find disconcerting is the very common practice of staring. Where frankly interested staring is considered very rude in some cultures, the Czechs are quite nonchalant about it. This could stem from the many hours that most Czechs spend on public transportation or from their relatively homogeneous culture, but whatever the reason, expect stares as a foreigner. It's easy to feel defensive or even insulted when someone stares at you, but it's generally not meant to be offensive. If it bothers you, simply smile at the person and he or she is likely to look away—or go back to their smartphone activities—almost immediately. Due to the sheer proliferation of cell phones and easily accessible Wi-Fi, staring is not as common as it once was, and many Czechs are just as likely, if not more so, to be fixated on their smartphone screens as they might be on their fellow passengers.

Czechs approach smiling the same way they do using the word "friend"—neither are thrown around lightly and without considered forethought. Many Czechs in fact see "excessive" smiling (as practiced by many North Americans, for example) as a sign of insincerity. Unless you are carrying a small dog in a shoulder bag or have a baby in a stroller, don't expect strangers to smile at you. This doesn't mean they are unfriendly, just that smiles are currency and they're going to spend it when it matters. You should feel free to smile when it seems natural to you—as in most places, it can go a long way toward smoothing interactions—but if it's not reciprocated, don't be upset.

On the matter of public transportation, the seats of street cars and buses that are reserved for the elderly, visually impaired, pregnant women, and parents with strollers are clearly marked and are to be respected. If you're sitting in one and someone in need comes aboard, you should surrender the seat even more quickly than you would a regular seat if you don't wish to be the subject of numerous disapproving gazes from your fellow passengers.

The acceptable boundaries of personal space in the Czech Republic, like the rest of Europe, are smaller than in North America simply because of the need to coexist in a confined space. Even so, away from public transportation and other crowded situations, Czechs appreciate having some extra personal space. As we've seen, they don't like a lot of physical contact with people they don't know really well and are most comfortable with at least 1.5 feet (0.5 meters) distance where possible.

Never put your feet on a seat or park bench, at least not in view of a *babička* (grandmother)—elderly ladies are the unofficial guardians of all that is right and proper in Czech culture and there hasn't yet been a security camera system devised that can catch the sort of details that a Czech granny can. If you raise the ire of a *babička*, you can expect to get an earful and she isn't going to care one bit that you don't understand a word she's saying.

THE MEDIA

Since about 2015, the Czech media has suffered a distinct drop in public confidence. While the Czech Republic ranked 40th in the World Press Freedom Index 2021, there are serious concerns about the ownership of a number of the nation's news outlets falling into the hands of a few wealthy tycoons with strong political connections.

The Czechs put most trust in their public broadcasters, both television and radio, for their news. The most popular news platforms are the Internet and television; radio is still popular, print media much less so. Facebook and Instagram are most popular among those who have social media accounts.

Where broadcast media is concerned, the major players are the state-owned Czech Television (Česká televize) and Czech Radio (Český rozhlas). Private television broadcasters of note are TV Nova and Prima televize. Private radio stations include Evropa 2, Frekvence 1, and Radio Impuls.

The press, which covers a broad political spectrum, includes serious journals such as *Mladá fronta DNES* (right-leaning), *Lidové noviny* (center-right), *Právo* (left-leaning), and *Hospodářské noviny* (economic news). There are also tabloids like *Blesk* and *Aha!*

The weekly news magazines *Respekt* and *Reflex* both cover current affairs, politics, economics, and other matters, at both domestic and international levels. *dTest* is a monthly consumer advocacy and product review magazine that enjoys wide popularity in the country.

IN TOUCH WITH THE OUTSIDE WORLD

Keeping up with world news or friends and family presents no challenge in the Czech Republic as international media—including cable news channels, foreign newspapers, and English-language journals—are widely available. Even in small towns it is generally possible to track down some form of international newspaper or a television with CNN or BBC, if you need a fix—and if you can't, there are few spots in the country without decent Internet coverage and Wi-Fi connection.

TELEPHONE

For visitors, making calls home is generally not a problem, although that becomes less true the farther you get from cities. Direct dialing from hotel or hostel landlines—assuming they allow you to—is not recommended because of high rates and surcharges. Landlines in general are very rare in the Czech Republic outside an office setting. Due to the high cost of landlines and the ubiquity of cell phones, landlines in Czech homes are almost unheard of these days.

Payphones are all but gone and, even if you find one, this is definitely not a recommended option—even for local, much less for international, calls. They eat coins at an obscene rate.

Cell phones really are a necessity here for local communication. There are three mobile providers in the Czech Republic: O2, T-Mobile, and Vodafone. It's best to check your roaming conditions with your own provider before embarking on your trip. It is also a good idea to check the Web sites of the local providers—all three have English-language options on their Web sites—to see what, if anything, you might need to do once you arrive. Depending on your planned length of stay, purchasing a local SIM card may be your best option.

INTERNET

Accessing the Internet is a breeze pretty much anywhere in the country. Internet penetration and cellular network coverage is around 100 percent. Texting is one of the most popular forms of electronic communication among Czechs and messaging apps such as WhatsApp are popular.

As Wi-Fi is virtually omnipresent, though not always free, checking e-mail and using your favorite Internet sites will not present a problem. Internet cafés can still be found, but they are rarer than they once were because most public areas have Wi-Fi. The Czechs are a tech savvy bunch, and you probably won't have too much trouble finding someone with enough English to help you get set up if you need it.

With Wi-Fi so widely available, the best options for contacting friends and family from abroad really are Internet-based methods such as Skype, Zoom, or the various social media Web sites and messaging apps.

MAIL

To send letters, packages, or postcards, you can either buy stamps from newsstands and drop them in one of the many orange Česká Pošta boxes, or visit the post office. For Czechs, the post office is not just a place to mail things, however, so be prepared for some confusion. At the post office people can pay bills, bank, get insurance, access notary services, and so on. Each function has its own window and trying to get a different service at the "wrong" window can be an exercise in futility.

At most larger post offices all the functions are listed on a machine that spits out a number ticket for customers. The numbers then come up on a main board and on electronic signs above the windows. Don't expect there to be any rhyme or reason to the order in which they appear; you might be in for a long wait even if it looks as though your number could be coming up soon.

Overall, the postal service is reasonably reliable, especially outgoing mail, although as in most places, sending items of high value or cash is inadvisable. DHL, Federal Express, and UPS all have a presence in the Czech Republic.

CONCLUSION

Whether standing in the wrong line at the post office or surveying a city or town from a vantage point, man-made or natural, there is something to be learned at every turn during a visit to the Czech Republic.

For the traveler who seeks more than what mere tourism provides, that learning process is what makes heading to foreign destinations special. To quote

Michael Palin, comedian, writer of many travel books, and host of many travel documentaries: "I've never particularly liked travelling with large groups or being told where to go by somebody else. I prefer to find out for myself."

While not all Czechs are entirely pleased that their country has become a popular tourist—and traveler—destination, they are uniformly proud of what it has to offer. With a little prompting and cultural sensitivity, they are happy to share it with informed visitors. Czechs have given the world some amazing gifts—from the invention of the word "robot" to the grit and determination of the inspirational runner and Olympic champion Emil Zátopek—and those contributions are likely to continue even as they integrate more closely into Europe and the world.

A visit to the Czech Republic will bring you face to face with a down-to-earth, well-educated group of people who are unpretentious, creative, and resilient. They have a layer of reserve that takes a bit of patience to cut through, but do so and your efforts will be rewarded with very good company and loyal friendship. The Czechs have an enviable joy for living, which many of them would never admit to. It's a side of them you will likely only see if you take the time to get to know them. If you take that time, you'll find it time well spent.

APPENDIX 1: SOME CZECH FIRSTS

1348 The first university in central Europe founded in Prague by Charles IV, King of Bohemia and Holy Roman Emperor; it is still known as Charles University (Univerzita Karlova).

1411 The first Czech translation of the Bible.

1519–20 The first dollars minted at Jáchymov (in German, Joachymsthal). These were the *Joachymsthaler Gulden* (Joachymsthal florins), the name of which became shortened to *Thaler*, Czech *tolar*, then spread throughout the Habsburg lands and across the world.

1754 Prokop Diviš (1696–1765) built the first lightning conductor at Přímětice, near Znojmo. He was working at the same time as, but independently of, Benjamin Franklin, who is also credited with the invention, the theory of which Diviš had published in 1753.

1790s František Ondřej Poupě (1753–1805), a brewmaster, revolutionized beer production. He was the first to apply scientific method to the brewing process. During the 1790s, he published a two-volume book that is regarded as the first scientfic work on beer production. He later wrote the first modern textbook on brewing. Many of the principles he established are still in use today.

1824–32 The first railway in continental Europe (initially horse-drawn) constructed between České Budějovice and Linz by František Antonín Gerstner (1795–1840), who also built the first Russian railway, from St. Petersburg to Tsarskoye Selo

1826 The first ship's propeller patented by Josef Ressel, a forester of Czech descent. It was first tested on a ship in Trieste in 1829.

1827 The first modern plow that broke up the earth as well as turning it over invented by the cousins František and Václav Veverka and first demonstrated at Lhota pod Libčany. Industrial manufacture began in 1849, the year the cousins died.

1865 The natural scientist and abbot of the Augustine monastery in Brno, Johann Gregor Mendel (1822–84), the founder of modern genetics, published his results on crossbreeding plants. He is usually regarded as Austrian, but the Czechs are nevertheless pleased to claim him on account of where he worked.

1927 Eliška Junková (1900–1994) was the first female racing driver to win a Grand Prix event when she took the title in the two-liter sports car class in Germany in 1927. Sometimes known as Elisabeth Junck.

1956 Otto Wichterle (1913–98), the chemist who co-created hydrogels and was the inventor of the first soft contact lenses based on them.

1966 The first Oscar awarded to a Czech(oslovak) film was for *Shop on Main Street*.

1984 Antonín Holý (1936–2012), the scientist who synthesized and patented Tenofovir, a key ingredient in some of the most effective medications against AIDS and HIV. Tenofovir is better known by trade names such as Truvada and Viread, among others.

2011 American-based Czech plastic surgeon, Bohdan Pomahač (1971–), performed the first full face transplant in the USA. The surgery was performed at Brigham and Women's Hospital in Boston.

2018 At the 2018 Winter Olympic Games in Pyeongchang, South Korea, Ester Ledecká (1995–) was the first person to win two gold medals in the same Winter Games in two disciplines—Super G in downhill skiing and the parallel double slalom in snowboarding. She also became the second woman in history to win Olympic gold in two disciplines.

APPENDIX 2: USEFUL APPS

Czech society is tech savvy and well connected online. Here are some international and homegrown apps that can be helpful to the visitor.

Cultural Activities

GoOut is a Czech-based app that helps you find cultural events around the country and buy tickets to them.

Ordering Groceries and Meals

Rohlik.cz is a popular homegrown grocery shopping app that allows you to do your grocery shopping online and have it delivered.

Dáme jídlo is a nationwide food ordering and delivery service with connections to over 2,000 restaurants across the country. The app gives you access to restaurant menus and allows you to pay for your order online. It works very well in larger centers and you can have your meal delivered to your home or office.

Wolt is a Finnish-based food ordering and delivery platform similar to Dáme jídlo.

Trip Planning and Navigation

IDOS is very useful for planning trips inside the country and to neighboring ones. It allows you to search for bus and train connections at local, regional, national, and international levels.

Mapy.cz is another highly recommended homegrown app. It is the Czech answer to Google Maps and is a product of Seznam.cz. While Google Maps is popular in the Czech Republic, Mapy.cz can often provide more detailed and up-to-date information in their maps of Czech localities.

Coach and Rail Transportation

Můj vlak is an app created by Czech Rail that allows you to plan your trip, purchase tickets, and check the real-time status of the trains involved in your trip as well as the stations involved.

RegioJet is an app created by Student Agency that will allow you to plan a trip and purchase tickets using the highly visible yellow trains and coaches they operate to destinations inside the country and farther afield in Europe.

Leo Express is a competitor to RegioJet and Czech Rail and have their own app to allow you to plan your trip and buy tickets using their trains and buses.

Flixbus is another competitor in the coach scene in the Czech Republic. The German company has an app to help you plan your trip and buy your tickets.

Bike Sharing and Ride Sharing

Liftago is useful if you need a ride to somewhere that public transportation can't take you or if you don't want to risk a taxi. Liftago operates in more than twenty localities around the country.

Nextbike is a German-based bike-sharing service that operates in thirteen municipalities around the country. Their app will help you locate one of their bike lockup stations near you and take you through the process of renting a bike through them.

Rekola is a Czech-based bike-sharing service operating in five Czech cities. They do not have dedicated bike lockup stations, so their app will help you to find one of their bikes near your location and take you through the process of renting it.

Weather Forecasts

Windy is a weather forecast app created by the founder of Seznam.cz.

Meteoradar is another Czech-based weather forecast app.

FURTHER READING

Askwith, Richard. *Today We Die a Little: Zátopek, Olympic Legend to Cold War Hero.* London: Vintage Books, 2016.

Čornej, Petr. *Great Stories in Czech history.* Translated by Anna Bryson. Prague: Práh, 2005.

Gerlach, David. *The Economy of Ethnic Cleansing: The Transformation of the German–Czech Borderlands after World War II.* Cambridge: Cambridge University Press, 2017.

Koutná, Kristýna. *Czech Cookbook Christmas Baking.* Brno: self-published, 2018.

Kuras, Benjamin. *Czechs and Balances: A Nation's Survival Kit.* Prague: Baronet, 1998.

Lyons, Pat and Rita Kindlerová (eds.). *Contemporary Czech Society.* Prague: Institute of Sociology of the Czech Academy of Sciences, 2016.

Owen, Jonathan L. *Avant-Garde to New Wave: Czechoslovak Cinema, Surrealism and the Sixties.* New York & Oxford: Berghahn Books, 2011.

Pánek, Jaroslav and Oldřich Tůma. *A History of the Czech Lands.* Prague: Karolinum, 2018.

Petrová, Sylva. *Czech Glass.* Prague: UMPRUM, 2018.

Rubeš, Janek and Honza Mikulka. *Honest Guide-Prague.* Prague: Cooboo, 2019.

Sebestyen, Victor. *Revolution 1989: The Fall of the Soviet Empire.* London: Phoenix, 2010.

Szczygiel, Mariusz. *Gottland: Mostly True Stories from Half of Czechoslovakia.* Translated by Antonia Lloyd-Jones. New York & London: Melville House Publishing, 2014.

Watson, Nicholas. *When Lions Roar.* Prague: Trinity Publications, 2014.

Whybray, Adam. *The Art of Czech Animation: A History of Political Dissent and Allegory.* London: Bloomsbury Publishing, 2020.

Web Sites

Czech Tourism	**visitczechrepublic.com**
Tres Bohemes	**tresbohemes.com**
Czech Film Review	**czechfilmreview.com**
Czech Cookbook	**czechcookbook.com**
Czech Gastronomy	**czechgastronomy.com**
Radio Prague International	**english.radio.cz**
Kafkadesk	**kafkadesk.org**
Brno Daily	**brnodaily.com**
Czech Class 101	**czechclass101.com**
SlowCZECH	**slowczech.com**

PICTURE CREDITS

Cover image: *View over the Old Town, Prague.* © Shutterstock by Oleksiy Mark.

Shutterstock: pages 15 by Kochneva Tetyana; 17 by DavidTB; 27 by zebra0209; 48 by svic; 72 by sebikus; 79 by cge2010; 86 by Roman Bjuty; 88 by haak78; 92 by lightpoet; 101 by Vladimir Hodac; 108 by Gonzalo Bell; 112 by Tatiana Dyuvbanova; 114 by Kojin; 124 by Vladimir Sazonov; 127 by Miroslav Hlavko; 130 (top left and bottom left) by Stepanek Photography; 130 (top right) by AS Food studio; 130 (bottom right) by JuliaWozniak; 133 (bottom left) by franz12; 138 by Luciano Mortula – LGM; 139 by tichr; 140 by DaLiu; 151 by Marsan; 155 by Ceri Breeze; 162 by Mike Mareen; 164 by David Jancik; 165 by alenacepl; 167 by Alexandra08; 180 by guruXOX.

Unsplash: pages 12 by Fredy Martinez; 106 by Kevin Andre; 144 by John Jacobson.

Pinterest: page 68 article by Stephanie Vlahos.

Creative Commons Attribution-Share Alike 4.0 International license: page 182 © Kychot.

Creative Commons Attribution-Share Alike 3.0 Unported license: pages 51 © Jorge Royan; 161 © Chmee2.

Creative Commons Attribution-Share Alike 3.0 Austria license: page 22 © Mikuláš Klimčák (artist), Peter Zelizňák (photo).

Creative Commons Attribution-Share Alike 2.5 Generic license: page 20 © Petr Novák, Wikipedia.

Creative Commons Attribution-Share Alike 2.0 Generic license: page 143 © s.yume

INDEX